PURSUING
THE
GOOD LIFE

**FROM
SURVIVING
TO
THRIVING**

DR. MARK J. BRITZMAN, ED.D.

Copyright © 2021 by Dr. Mark J. Britzman, Ed.D.

All rights reserved. No part of this publication may be reproduced, distributed or transmitted in any form or by any means, including photocopying, recording or other electronic or mechanical methods, without the prior written permission of the publisher, except in the case of brief quotations embodied in reviews and certain other non-commercial uses permitted by copyright law.

Printed in the United States of America

Print ISBN: 978-1-953910-22-6
E-Book ISBN: 978-1-953910-23-3

Canoe Tree Press

4697 Main Street
Manchester Center, VT 05255

Canoe Tree Press is a division of DartFrog Books.

Contents

Introduction 5
Chapter 1: Improving Our Moral Landscape 11
Chapter 2: What Is the Good Life? 33
Chapter 3: Developing a Capacity for Delight 49
Chapter 4: Nourishing Important Relationships 69
Chapter 5: Moving Toward Wellness 75
Chapter 6: Finding Meaning in Work 89
Chapter 7: Making Our World a Better Place 103
Chapter 8: Jump-Starting Positive Changes 117
Chapter 9: Conclusion 127
References 133
About the Author 139

Introduction

The story of your life is unfolding. There are no inconsequential choices, meaningless moments, or disposable days. This book is an invitation to step out of survival mode and move toward a compelling narrative where you are thriving in life. The adventure entails cultivating key character traits that will unleash your gifts and talents in a manner that inspires hope and possibilities, moving you toward increased well-being, meaning, and purpose in your life.

The candle of our lives is burning. Many of us have more yesterdays than tomorrows, and it becomes imperative to set yourself up to have the best day possible. The process of seizing  the day necessitates an inner strength that is fortified by developing a positive mindset, cultivating a healthy support system, and treating your mind, body, and soul with compassion, loving-kindness, and respect. Positivity is the key to transform your thoughts, self-statements, and belief system into an "I got this, let's go" attitude.

Thankfully, tiny changes can ripple into a significant life transformation. The key to effective change is having a vision and a goal for self-improvement and emphasizing the optimal process that jump-starts you into action. A small behavior change can lead to a cascade of successes. In contrast, doing more of the same can often lead to missed opportunities and regret. Your daily habits can be your gift or curse. The key to developing healthy habits is often planting a seed that emanates from one small choice or shift sustained over time. The benefits of lively change compounds into significant consequences in all major life tasks.

Developing a sense of gratitude generates positive feelings related to focusing on what is going right in life. Social connections are a vital ingredient for feeling a deep sense of significance and belonging. Meditative moments can occur when you embrace opportunities to fully accept the present moment, noticing what is right in the world. Allowing yourself time to take a break allows your body to reset and move toward renewal. Physical movement enhances your mood and elevates your immune response. Healthy nutritional choices fuel your mind, body, and soul. Seizing opportunities to help others with compassion, kindness, and altruism provides us with a sense of connection to something bigger than ourselves.

Pursuing the good life necessitates a vision for what we want in life. An optimal direction can be established and guides choices to fulfill needs related to love, belonging, significance, freedom, and fun. Your ability to self-evaluate the emotional consequences related to your attitude and behavioral choices will help you choose a path that allows you to experience more joy and inner peace.

Life is an incredible adventure that provides us with numerous choices throughout each day. Multiple opportunities and challenges will yield positive and negative consequences, some being significant. Our world is a noisier place, and likely numerous demands are competing for your time at this very moment. Texts, tweets, emails, birthday notifications, internet search opportunities, and new posts are waiting for you. Your response will be tabulated by a supercomputer that will record the data and learn with advanced algorithms to understand and manipulate your behavior and spending habits in the future. More importantly, you have family, relatives, and friends trying to connect with you and want a response as soon as possible. The technological advances serve many useful purposes but necessitate a need for clarity, focus, and prioritization to live a life in concert with what is truly most important to you. There is a cost to your well-being when attention becomes hijacked on something that is not essential. Feelings of anxiety have become the norm and are linked to a focus on the next thing that could go wrong.

The contents of this book intend to help you interrupt unhealthy patterns of thinking and behaving and jumpstart a journey on an exciting path of possibilities to stretch the edges of your potential and pursue the best life possible. Developing a more extraordinary ability to control your focus with a positive, flexible, and determined mind is the foundation to create a vision and plan for developing improved character, relationships, wellness, and tapping a deeper and more significant meaning and purpose in your life. This journey begins with your relationship with yourself.

I want to introduce myself. My name is Mark J. Britzman. By profession, many individuals refer to me as Dr. Mark as I am a licensed psychologist and former full-tenured professor in counselor education. I have traveled throughout the United States and beyond with the hope of improving our moral landscape via providing workshops on character education and promoting healthier, more cooperative, and respectful relationships. I am blessed to have a wonderful family and now reside in the beautiful Black Hills of South Dakota that provides daily and epic opportunities to be inspired by nature. I try to personally spend as much time outdoors

INTRODUCTION

as possible walking, hiking, and snowshoeing, noticing and then capturing what is right and beautiful in our world, facilitated by a passion for photography. Thus, you will find many pictures in this book that may appear random, which they are, but will hopefully stimulate your present attention and focus on a way that generates positive feelings. I continue to actualize my potential but fully realize that I have many growth areas in my life, and self-improvement is a process.

I am deeply motivated by helping individuals, couples, and families each week by offering counseling that focuses on hope, positivity, authenticity, effort, mindfulness, and minimizing an over-emphasis on psychopathology. My  gifts and character strengths include deep compassion and thirst for bringing out the best in others via a keen perceptiveness, the ability to help others feel deeply heard, and a strong belief that choices matter.

This book intends to stretch your comfort zone by promoting self-evaluation of your vision for the best life possible and make adjustments to your attitude, thoughts, and behaviors that preserve your integrity while propelling you to pursue the best experience possible.

Chapter 1

Improving Our Moral Landscape

Do you have a fantastic person in your life who is an everyday hero? These individuals often march into the trenches of our lives without a drumbeat but leave a legacy that endures forever. Our everyday heroes somehow learned that living a life that matters necessitate being trustworthy, respectful, caring, fair, responsible, and generous. They seem to live according to their values and do the right thing even if no one is looking or costs them more than they want to pay.

Dealing with adversity consistently tests our character. Life is not fair, and bad things happen to good people. However, we always have a choice regarding how we respond. A person of character appears to focus on what they can control. There is a sense of gratitude as they have developed

a capacity of delight and appreciation, focusing on what is right in their life.

Do you believe there is a growing hole in our moral ozone? Ethical issues confront us every day, such as: being asked to lie for a friend, passing along a juicy piece of gossip, finding ourselves in a conversation with a bigot, receiving too much change at the store, using our position to take advantage of an employee, treating others in a way we would not tolerate for ourselves, being "creative" with work reports or accounting. These acts may be perceived as moral misdemeanors when compared to other offenses. Bad choices are exacerbated if alcohol or drugs are used as they contaminate one's judgment and ability to do the right thing. We will all make mistakes with potentially harmful consequences. However, would you do the same thing again?

The real ethical character test is whether we are willing to do the right thing even when it is not in our self-interest or when making the right decision costs more than we want to pay. One of the most significant obstacles to being a person of character and leading an ethical life is the dominance of self-centered, pleasure-seeking values: doing what makes us "feel good," satisfying our passions and urges, and avoiding pain and discomfort at all costs. The morally mature individual finds happiness in grander pursuits than the temporary pleasure produced by money, status, or popularity. That is why individuals who know the good, love the good, and do the good demonstrate their character's strength every day.

Protecting our moral landscape is linked to an increase in ethical behavior, and the benefits will produce positive consequences in our families, with our neighbors, and at our workplace. We simply must seize opportunities to bring out the best in others. Seemingly, actions speak louder than words, and many individuals who have tremendous character do the right thing consistently. Their skills are often groomed when nobody is watching, regardless of feeling tired or distressing. Individuals that possess unique character have a deep commitment to ethical values. What would the world look like if we raised the moral bar in society?

Imagine if people were more trustworthy. Personal disclosure would be much more honest and authentic, and relationships would vastly improve.

Individuals would feel much better because of authentically sharing their thoughts and feelings. Simultaneously, the listener would not have to expend energy figuring out what the person was saying. People would keep their promises. There would be less doubt regarding commitment, follow-up, arrival and departure times, and faithfulness. Loyalty would be more common, and individuals could confront interpersonal conflicts more proactively and foster solutions and an action plan. Integrity would spread, as thoughts, words, and deeds would be in concert with every relationship being sustained with a more significant commitment to loyalty and fidelity.

What would the world look like if there were more respect? Everyone would treat others as social equals regardless of physical appearance, race, cultural differences, sexual orientation, gender, or age. People would better tolerate differences of opinion. Condescending remarks would cease, while active listening would become more prevalent in every conversation. Good manners would be ubiquitous, and there would be less prejudice, harassment, manipulation, or coercion. Respect entails honoring the individual's worth and dignity of others, showing courtesy and civility, honoring reasonable social standards and customs, living by the Golden Rule, accepting differences, judging on character and ability, respecting the autonomy of others, and avoiding actual or threatened violence.

Imagine if each of us had a more profound commitment to responsible decision-making. Responsibility entails being accountable, exercising self-control, setting goals, and choosing a positive attitude. There would be an emphasis on doing one's duty, being self-reliant, pursuing excellence, being  proactive, being persistent, reflective, setting a good example, and being morally autonomous. Every individual would be more responsible for managing their time in harmony with their priorities, including their spiritual, emotional, and physical well-being. Healthy choices would be more common. Laziness and indifference would decline. The world would reap higher productivity rewards with people flourishing by using their gifts to benefit society.

What would the world look like if there were more fairness? An equal opportunity would exist for more people. Oppression would decline, increasing efforts toward more open trade and access to food, shelter, and technology. More evaluations would be made on relevant criteria in school and higher education in the workplace. Fairness describes a process and outcome that necessitates impartiality, thorough gathering of facts, and considering all perspectives before making a judgment. Cooperation, interdependence, and charitable giving would increase, and more nations would have access to education and decent employment. The consequences of undesirable behavior would be more consistent and fitting.

Imagine what the world would look like if there were more kindness, caring, and compassion; people would seek out more ways to make a positive difference in others' lives. Uncaring and hurtful remarks would decline. More people would thrive in life, and there would be no abuse, neglect, and loneliness. Wellness, positive energy, and an increased passion for life would be the byproduct of a more caring climate.

What would the world look like if there were more commitment to altruism, generosity, and good citizenship? Individuals would seize opportunities to bring out the best in others. People would vote for a higher number of politicians on appropriate criteria. Legislators would pass better laws that were in the best interests of everyone. A growing number of schools would connect more students with better teachers, curricula would be better researched, and the students would have a more excellent opportunity to learn. Roads would be safer in all weather conditions. There would be more improved law enforcement to protect the safety of citizens. Parks would be clean, and there would exist an unwavering commitment to protecting our environment.

Your character is a healing response to personal and social dysfunction and a function of your values. However, it is helpful to differentiate between ethical and non-ethical values. Ethical values are what we believe are essential regarding right and wrong, based on moral duty and virtues. Think  about why we get upset when we tell a lie or are lied to. Most often, it is because trust and honesty are essential to us. They are part of our ethical values.

Many of our values are how we think things should be if the world were run according to us. We know that life does not operate this way, but we still find ourselves frustrated when what we think is essential is ignored or overlooked by others or by circumstances. Values are often ranked by importance. These rankings are subjective and based on our preferences, which determines our priorities.

Values are what we feel are essential, so they shape our lives' goals and how we measure our success or failure. How we define ourselves in any situation depends on our values. It does not matter what others may say about our achievements. Our values determine how we view our accomplishments and failures.

Ethics is not about the way things are. It is about the way things ought to be. Ethics is a set of standards of duty and virtue, and right and wrong indicate how we should behave. Values determine what is important to us; ethical standards guide how we ought to pursue our goals. For example, we may like or value money or good grades. But do we gain them honorably or by cheating? Our ethics are the expression of how we pursue our values. Ethics has three equally important aspects; discerning right from wrong, concerned with stakeholders, and the discipline to do the right thing.

First, discernment is a recognition of what is right. It can be challenging since the ethical principles do not always yield a single moral choice. Often there is more than one "right" way to respond. Stakeholders are all those affected by our ethical decisions. We do not always arrive at justice in proper behavior by considering just the interaction between two people. We must often consider the impact on others. We also need the discipline to do what is right, regardless of temptations and pressures to do otherwise. We must recognize the difference between stated and operational values. Stated values are what we believe are essential. Operational values are revealed by our actions and decisions and how we resolve conflicts between competing values. Consistency between stated and operational values is a crucial ingredient of integrity.

Most of us are ethical in our own eyes. However, the real test is doing the right thing, perhaps when no one is looking, or if the cost is more than we want to pay. Ethics is about doing the right thing, but sometimes it can be about self-restraint and not doing anything. An act is not proper simply because it is permissible or legal; sometimes, we should not do what we have the power to do.

Ethics is about doing more than necessary because it is the right thing to do. Compliance is about doing what you are required to do by the laws or rules. An ethical person often chooses to do more than the law requires, and less than the law allows. Ethics goes beyond just compliance. Ethics is also not about self-interest. Many people adopt a live-and-let-live attitude about behavior; "I'll do whatever I want to do, and please don't judge me, and I won't judge you." Decision-making is reduced to risk and reward calculation; if the risk is low enough or the rewards are high enough, they can scrap ethical principles and do what they think will benefit themselves most immediately. Many people will cheat on exams, distort resumes, or falsify facts at work if they are never caught. So, self-interest ethics may seem to work at least in the short run, but the

long-term risks are loss of trust, broken relationships, and missed opportunities. Ironically, such a focus on self-interest is not in our best interest. Furthermore, what we say and do affects others around us. We all teach the values we demonstrate with our choices, attitude, and behavior, but our ethical character's real test is whether we are willing to do the right thing even when it may not be in our best interest.

Some people believe that the pursuit of happiness is moral, and they argue that we should pursue whatever makes us feel better. This is not unreasonable or unethical enough unless applied without regard to how others are affected by how we seek our happiness. One of the most significant obstacles to be in a person of character and leading an ethical life is the dominance of self-centered, pleasure-seeking values. The mature moral individual finds happiness and grander pursuits, making the world a slightly better place, and chooses not to be tempted by seeking temporary pleasure fueled by greed and hedonism.

So why be ethical? Virtue is its own reward. True self-esteem comes from the confidence and experience gained from accomplishing a task. Knowing that we have done the right thing makes us feel good about ourselves. Additional benefits are the admiration and fondness of loved ones and the respect of peers. It is also a wise thing to do. Mark Twain once said if you tell the truth, you do not have to remember anything. In the long run, being ethical is more straightforward, if not always more comfortable.

Many choose to be ethical for religious reasons. Our conscience is our internal source of proper judgment. A working conscience makes us aware of our conduct's moral aspect, and it urges us to prefer right over wrong. If character is defined by how we act when we think no one is watching, conscience is the inner force that is always observing and listening. Reputation is what other people think you are. It is something most all of us all care about. However, reputation is not character. Think about Abraham Lincoln's formulation, "Character is like a tree and reputation like a shadow. The shadow is what we think of it; the tree is the real thing." The tree is stable, but the shadow's shape and length depend on the light's angle. If we pay too much attention to our reputation, we could lose sight of our character.

Does personal discipline relate to whether our choices are rational or emotional? Have we considered the possible consequences to ourselves and others? Have we considered our long-term goals? It is easy to act impulsively. It is hard to pause and learn the habit of thinking a situation through before committing. We must also monitor and cultivate our thoughts. An adage warns us not to hang around with negative people. Negative people are particularly good at seeing what is wrong and how any perceived solutions are not attainable. What is worse is that we end up sounding and acting just like them if we associate with them long enough. There is an old saying that goes, "Watch your thoughts. They become words. Watch your words; they become actions. Watch your actions; they become habits. Watch your habits because they become your character. Watch your character; it becomes your destiny." If we fill our minds with me-only or whatever it takes to get ahead, we should not be surprised if their choices follow. We should examine the thoughts that pop into our heads the next time an opportunity or temptation comes our way.

What do we believe about our values, our priorities, and our ethics? How can they be adjusted to reflect a stronger sense of what is right and wrong? Changing the way we think is the first big step toward improving our character. It takes courage to live up to ethical principles. When we start new ways of responding and behaving, suddenly we find ourselves in unknown territory, and it can become frightening.

Courage is not the absence of fear; it is learning to control a concern instead of letting the fear control us. It takes courage to work on our character continually. Strange things happen when we change; the people we associate with will also often change too. It takes courage to continue working on our character when others are pressing us to stay as we were.

Finally, good character is developed with determination. As with any new activity, we will make a lot of mistakes at the beginning. We will feel the pull of old habits and ways of thinking and telling us to respond in old familiar ways. And do not forget those friends and family members who respond to us according to our former character. Determination to be better, to improve our character, is necessary to be successful.

Although pursuing our interests comes naturally, we must also make ethical decisions and consider others' interests and our choices' long-term implications. Such a decision-making process does not come naturally. We must model, teach, and nurture good character at home primarily and in the areas of education, community life, and the workplace.

To understand the fundamental importance of character, we should ask ourselves some questions: Would we rather be married to someone we trust or not? Would we rather our coworkers or neighbors respect us or not? Would we prefer our children to be responsible or irresponsible? Do we want a just society? Would we want to fly on an airplane whose pilots cheated on their training exams? Would you like to have surgery conducted by a doctor who faked his or her way through medical school? We all would like others to have good character. But we must remember: the best place to start is with ourselves, which always remains the most significant challenge.

Reasonable people can disagree about many things. However, there seem to be principles that become the law of the land and serve as a springboard for making ethical decisions. For instance, who would be offended by the following values: trustworthiness, respect, responsibility, fairness, caring, and altruism?

How can you help create a culture where character still matters? Environmental awareness entails a concern for others. Developing a healthy community appears to be linked to an increase in moral behavior, and the benefits are often evident with loved ones, friends, colleagues, and neighbors. We, too, often minimize the importance of ordinary people who consistently try to do the right thing even when there is a cost (Britzman and Hanson 2005).

Our interpersonal relationships are enriched when we genuinely care about another person's perspective and communicate in a manner that reflects a sense of caring, respect, and empathy. "Your odds of being happy increase by 15 percent if a direct connection in your social network is happy. In other words, having direct and frequent social contact with someone who has high well-being dramatically boosts your chances of being happy" (Fredrickson 2009, 34).

How do you make the best ethical decision? We have so many choices to make each day. Most are trivial, but some have the potential to have momentous consequences for the stakeholders—those affected by our decision—the greater the potential consequences, the greater the need for careful decision-making. To evaluate the seriousness of any critical choice, ask yourself the following: Could it cause physical harm to you or anyone else? How would the decision affect your reputation? Would your choice bring other individuals closer or further away from you? How does your current choice impact your direction toward goals and your vision for a good life?

Recognizing a serious decision alone is not enough. We still need to make the best choice that achieves the desired outcomes. Will the choice made strengthen your overall character and commitment to values, including but not limited to trustworthiness, respect, responsibility, fairness, caring, and altruism? Ethical decisions necessitate discernment and the willingness to do the right thing that may produce consequences greater than we want to pay.

How will this choice help or hurt others?

Is my decision in concert with my commitment to being trustworthy, respectful, responsible, caring, fair, and altruistic?

If this decision necessitates a conflict in my values, what choice produces the most considerable amount of good?

Treating others with respect is the foundation of good character and is the springboard of making an ethical decision. We need this commitment regardless if we agree with the person or hold him or her in high esteem. Also, it is crucial to make a choice that highlights and models your commitment to critical values. If values conflict with each other, what choice produces the most considerable amount of good?

One must stop and think before a choice and think ahead. First, it is necessary to prevent the momentum of events long enough to permit calm analysis. This may require discipline, but it is a powerful antidote against poor choices. The challenge is that many decisions can temporarily enhance short-term mood, which often serves as an illusion but will produce many negative consequences. Choosing to over-indulge with food, sex, alcohol, and drugs may be compelling in the short-term but have negative and life-changing implications for the rest of your life.

Feelings of unworthiness and alienation can thwart our essential goodness and inherent tendency to thrive in life. Unhealthy compensation for feelings of inferiority sets the stage for poor choices that provide short-term respite from suffering but lead to long-term negative consequences. Attempts to cope and just survive the day becomes a goal as feelings of worry and anxiety develops a moral fog and resulting feelings of depressed mood. Many try to outrun or maneuver negative emotions by keeping busy and developing a keen eye for others' flaws. Others avoid and isolate, which serves as an illusion to prevent negative emotions but sets the stage for profound loneliness.

It is easy for any of us to employ rationalizations to try and justify doing the wrong thing. There, of course, are always others who are worse.

"You think I am bad, what about…"
"Well, it is not illegal to…"
"It is not my job to…"
"I was just doing it for you."
"Sometimes you have to fight fire with fire."
"It is not going to hurt anyone if I…"
"Everyone else is doing it."
"There was nothing in it for me."
"You know I deserved to…"
"I can make up for it."
"It does not mean that I cannot…"

Rational decisions are the result of a careful reasoning process, evaluating the effectiveness and ethics of options. Rationalizations arise to justify choices the decision-maker wants to make or has already made. You face myriad challenges every day that test the strength of your character.

In the last century, seminal thinkers warned of the erosion of character. Alfred Adler, the Austrian psychiatrist whose ideas have gained influence since his death, stated that "social interest," regarding others' concerns, was the best barometer of mental health. Dr. Adler held that behavior is always purposeful and socially embedded. As a result, it is essential to be socially responsible, cooperative, and altruistic and encouraged to make useful choices to achieve feelings of significance and belong (Carlson and Maniacci 2012). American psychologist Abraham Maslow concurred, stating, "The ultimate disease of our time is valuelessness." Lawrence Kohlberg, the famed developmental psychologist, also rejected the moral vacuity of values clarification and sought to help young people with the process of making ethical decisions (Britzman and Hanson 2005). "If we, as parents, educators, and community members don't solve this character deficit problem," wrote David Brooks and Frank Goble, "we are doomed to live with the consequences. If we think that teen pregnancy, gangs, and alcohol abuse, school failure, a loss of civility, the lack of work ethic, and violence are the problem, then we are doomed to live with these symptoms" (1997, 120).

In every relationship, one's character will matter! Will the world be better off because of your existence? Are you willing to consistently do the right thing even in the face of temptation and adversity? What will be your legacy? These are difficult questions to consider because our daily lives have become increasingly cluttered with endless "to do" lists. Too many people heed the message that they should get ahead in life at all costs. Unrestrained competitiveness is often the nemesis of moral living, promoting the illusion of gaining a meaningful experience via the accumulation of wealth and material things. This selfish mentality is an enemy of integrity. Doing the right thing is relatively easy if it seems to serve one's purposes to do so. But what if being ethical comes with a price? Persons of excellent character are, of course, not perfect. It is easy to rationalize that I am not so bad if others are worse. However, they own up to learn from past mistakes and work hard to do better the next day. Anyone can live a life of significance by consistently making a positive difference in the lives of others. First, do no harm; secondly, be good; and lastly, be happy.

Does being an everyday hero and pursuing the good life seem overwhelming to you? It is easy to overestimate the cost of doing the right thing and under-

estimate failing to do so. Keep in mind that you do not have to be perfect, gifted, rich, great-looking, or have high self-esteem to be a person of character.

An everyday hero leaves a beautiful legacy that will last forever. Their altruistic spirits provide daily opportunities to bring out the best in themselves and others. People of character instill a sense of hope, affirmation, and encouragement that the human spirit is compassionate and generous. They take personal responsibility for living lives of character, treating themselves and others with love, care, and respect while remaining mindful of a broader purpose of being trustworthy, fair, and good citizens. Their purpose in life is fueled by a zest for living and a commitment to proactively go after life. The byproduct of their exuberance for living is a positive energy that radiates to others in the form of encouragement. Life is a precious gift. I hope that your presence will leave a legacy of greater compassion for others, respect for diversity, and relationships strengthened with integrity.

The following poem was written by Michael Josephson, founder, and president of CHARACTER COUNTS! and a wonderful mentor in my life.

"The older I get, the less I know, but I know some things:

I know that I am a work in progress, and there will always be a gap between who I am and who I want to be.

I know that I do not have to be sick to get better and that every day brings opportunities to improve my life and my character.

I know that it's easier to talk about integrity than to live it and that the true test is my willingness to do the right thing even when it costs more than I want to pay.

I know that character is more important than competence.

I know that it takes years to build up trust and only seconds to destroy it.

I know that I often judge myself by my intentions and most noble acts, but that my last worst act will judge me.

I know that I cannot control what will happen to me but that I have a lot to say about what happens to me.

I know that pain is inevitable, but suffering is optional.

I know that attitudes, both good and bad, are contagious.

I know that winning is more than coming in first and that there is no real victory without honor.

I know that it takes a conscientious effort to be kind, but that kindness changes lives.

I know that neither gratitude nor forgiveness comes naturally; both often require acts of will.

I know and that I am generally as happy as I am willing to be.

I know that the surest road to happiness is that real success is being significant.

I know that happiness is deeper and more enduring than either pleasure or fun and that I am generally as happy as I am willing to be.

I know that the surest road to happiness is good

relationships and that the best way to have good relationships is to be a good person."

Chapter 2

What Is the Good Life?

It is perfectly normal for you to ask, "My life is all right, but is this as good as it gets? Why don't I feel happier?" This mindset is often followed by blaming yourself for not being more positive. "I could be living in a third-world country with famine and disease. What is wrong with me?" You then begin to worry and borrow imagined problems from the future. If you feel this way, you are not alone. Most people want to be happier but perhaps get lost in a hectic world.

Positive psychology is often described as the scientific study of what makes life worth living, providing insight into the direct impacts of joy, happiness, and quality of life. "What is good in life is not simply the absence of what is problematic" (Peterson 2013, 4). Many of us struggle with an onslaught of items added to our to-do list. "I should check my email, return some of my voicemail messages, get some groceries, do some cleaning, prepare for the upcoming week, make sure the car is maintained, and so on." Minor tasks flow into your life, and sometimes significant distress can also arrive without notice. There appears no reprieve unless you take a nap, and if you do, you may suffer from a tinge of guilt. Life becomes a treadmill that never stops, and the goal is just to survive the week.

Pursuing the good life entails clarifying your hopes and dreams, finding an optimal direction that moves you closer to what you want, self-evaluating the consequences of your choices, and consistently developing a plan that is need-fulfilling. Drawing from counseling and psychology has reinforced the ingredients necessary to generate positive feelings and heightened well-being. Peterson (2013) describes significant factors that contribute to psychological health and pursuing a good life, including but not limited to, the following:

- Experiencing more positive feelings than negative feelings
- Being satisfied with life
- Identifying and using talents and strengths
- Becoming engaged in healthy activities
- Having close relationships with neighbors, colleagues, friends, and family members
- Being a contributing member of a social community
- Having a purpose (19).

Every choice you make has a consequence. Your total behavior consists of thinking, doing, feeling, and physiology. You have the most control over your thinking and behaving. However, all domains are interdependent (Glasser 2011; Wubbolding 2010).

Your journey can be fueled by making healthy choices related to your wellness, which helps you develop greater resilience and ability to handle adversity and distress and creates additional positive energy to thrive in life rather than survive the day.

However, if making the necessary choices that increase happiness were easy, everyone would be pursuing a life that leads to sustained joy rather than short-term pleasure. Temporary mood enhancers are available throughout any day. Too often, overindulgence in alcohol, drugs, overspending, and overeating, among other vices, serve as fool's gold, with no sustaining value but instead casts an illusion of a temporary haven for feeling better. The inevitable emotional crash often creates a greater need to look for another quick fix to feel better. Of course, psychologists have a fancy word phrase to describe this process, called the hedonistic treadmill. You want to feel better now, but you are going nowhere that produces long-term, sustained happiness.

Sadly, many people just try to get through each day by seeking temporary joy or diversions. Ultimately, unhealthy choices lead to a host of mental health disorders, including but not limited to anxiety and depression. Negative emotions can call out what is not working for you and provide opportunities to make better choices, perhaps even a new life path. We all have made poor choices, and lessons can be learned from the bad times in life that may also toughen us up and allow us to become more resilient to adversity and possibly a higher capacity of delight when choosing to make life better.

According to Ben-Shahar (2007), the rate of depression is ten times higher today than in the 1960s. Is this based solely on our physiology's erosion and attributed to poor brain chemistry linked to living in a faster-paced society?

Do you believe happiness is a choice? How much of good feelings are generated by your perception of the quality of your life? Researchers have recently defined happiness as the radiation of joy over one's entire existence or a deep sense of flourishing that arises from making healthy choices.

Shawn Anchor, the author of *The Happiness Advantage* and a former instructor at Harvard, studies the science of happiness. He claims you can change your health, relationships, work, energy, and life in general by becoming more optimistic. He believes positivity is the fuel that impacts every aspect of your life.

Many self-experts claim this, but there is a hollowness without valid and reliable research. For instance, longitudinal studies were done of nuns who wrote down their perceptions of their lives in the 1930s. By the way, nuns are a fantastic experimental group because their days are somewhat uniform regarding dress, nutrition, and daily rituals. Their logs were then objectively analyzed by a team of researchers and categorized into areas of happiness based on their journal entries. Interestingly, 54 percent of the so-called happy nuns lived to age ninety-four, while only 15 percent of the unhappy nuns lived to age ninety-four (Anchor 2013).

What are you doing when you experience feelings of sustained happiness? There is a high likelihood that you are most content with your life when you make choices that satisfy basic needs. However, do you know what these needs are, and if so, do you have a vision and plan to make consistent choices to ensure feeling good about your life?

There appear to be basic human needs that are universal. There is a high likelihood that these needs are genetically programmed and are with us from birth until death. These needs, when satisfied, can lead to feelings of happiness and joy. Conversely, painful emotions are universal when the needs are not met consistently.

Human beings are incredibly resilient. Our physiology is programmed to live a long life, depending on our genetic makeup and choices to promote or deter our overall sense of wellness. Furthermore, the need is not only to survive but to thrive. A central basic need is for love and belonging. Some of your most satisfying experiences likely entail interacting with those whom you respect and admire.

In contrast, some of your most painful memories probably are associated with times when you were criticized, blamed, or put down by others. In an optimal environment, we seem to naturally want to make choices that enhance our sense of significance and feelings of self-worth. It feels good to be recognized and admired for who we are as well as our accomplishments.

We also need the freedom to control our lives and make choices without coercion, threats, or bribery from others or the external world. It feels good to be in control of our destiny. Freedom is intimately linked to internal motivation.

Lastly, we require fun and enjoyment. Life appears to be more demanding as one goes through childhood, adolescence, and enters adulthood. The careless joy, laughter, and permission to allow us to enjoy increasing life demands, responsibilities often trump the moment, and there is a tendency to worry and ruminate about the future. Consequently, the need for fun goes unfulfilled unless you choose time for activities, hobbies, and leisure pursuits that you enjoy. It is said that too many of us do not seize opportunities for enjoyable activities for various reasons, including but not limited to lack of time or perhaps feeling guilty that we should be doing something else on our endless to-do lists (Glasser 2011; Wubbolding 2010).

Perhaps meeting basic needs seems very self-serving, superficial, and even indulgent. If you believe I left out something fundamental, you are both right and wrong. You are right in the sense that I did not specifically mention the need for spirituality and faith. Ironically, the search for love, the desire for significance, and the yearning for freedom from external control are essential in your quest to deepen your purpose and meaning as you pursue the good life.

You can undoubtedly change your circumstances, especially if you are in a very unsatisfying location, relationship, or job. However, external factors contribute only a small percentage to your overall happiness; many researchers believe approximately 10 percent of your broad sense of well-being is linked to external factors unless you live in poverty, ravaged by addictions, or in a significant disrespectful relationship. You also have a genetic tendency related to your temperament and disposition, but you can change your brain. Even identical twins, which on average, are remarkably similar, can have variance regarding the way they experience their world and life (Anchor 2013).

Thriving in life and resulting feelings of happiness and well-being is a choice that facilitates movement toward pursuing the good life. Peterson (2013) stated that recent research reveals the following: Most people are generally happy. Happiness often begets more satisfaction, leading to desirable outcomes in school, work, fulfilling social relationships, and even good health and a longer lifespan on average.

Most people are resilient and bounce back from adversity.

Happiness strengthens character, which leads to positive relationships and helps serve as a buffer against the discouraging impact of disappointments and setbacks.

The strength of one's character is often revealed during times of crisis.

Other people matter, and relationships are the primary influencers of a meaningful life.

Spirituality and religion matter.

Satisfying work can provide greater meaning and purpose.

Money makes an ever-diminishing contribution to well-being unless it is used charitably to help others.

The "heart" matters more than the "head," and educators must focus not only on critical thinking but also on teaching unconditional caring and kindness.

Good days typically entail a sense of autonomy, competence, accomplishment, and positive connection with others.

Self-evaluation becomes a skill that allows you to understand your choices' consequences and overall direction in life.

Physical activity initiates a cascade of successes throughout the day.

Develop the capacity of delight via meditation, prayer, relaxation, or just deep breathing and focus on the present or what is right in your life.

Enriched relationships are the primary key related to fullness in life.

The good life can be taught!

Find a field of study or work that matters to you. (Anchor 2013; Ben-Shahar 2007; Fredrickson 2009; Glasser 2011, Meyers 2000; Peterson 2013; Rath 2007; Ricard 2011; Wubbolding 2010).

Pursuing the good life can begin by taking an inventory of what is going well in your life presently. Counting your blessings and not your afflictions has both practical value and research support (Wubbolding 2010). However, it necessitates taking an inventory of life, slowing down, and noticing what is right or even beautiful to pursue the good life.

How do you know what choices are linked to short-term pleasure or long-term sustained joy? Seemingly too many people look for temporary highs, such as alcohol, drugs, sex without love, and so on, because it gives them a momentary rush of pleasure. When asked why they engage in these behaviors, they will likely tell you it is fun, and they want to have a good time and feel good. The intense pleasure will evaporate, leaving a sense of emptiness and perhaps shame that sets the stage for searching for a more powerful quick fix to feel better.

Although life is often challenging and bad things can happen to good people like you, it is possible to positively react to adversity with effort, grit, and determination. Your journey is also facilitated by enjoying present moments, strengthening character, enriching relationships, and making healthy and need-fulfilling choices each day. You can then reap the consequences of greater meaning, purpose, and sustained joy.

Try to imagine what would make you happier.

A 70" improved 5K high-definition television with surround sound?

A new car?

Living in a warm climate?

Winning the lottery?

Retirement?

Perhaps a few readers remember what life was like in the 1940s. Approximately one-third of homes did not have running water, indoor toilets, a bathtub, or shower, and more than half had no central heating.

WHAT IS THE GOOD LIFE?

Sixty percent of adults over twenty-five years of age had an eighth-grade education, with only 25 percent earning a high school degree and only 5 percent graduating from college.

Now, compare that with living in today's world, where the typical household has running water, at least two bathrooms, and central heating, and is typically equipped with microwave ovens, dishwashers, smart televisions, personal computers, iPads, Kindles, Alexa, Siri, and, of course, cell phones.

When asked to rate their happiness level, individuals living in the 1940s reported being "very happy," with an average score of 7.5 on a ten-point scale. The average rating today is 7.2. Hmm. Why don't all these extra gadgets and luxuries make us significantly happier?

Sonja Lyumbomirsky (2007), an internationally renowned social psychologist and author of *The How of Happiness: A Scientific Approach to Getting the Life You Want*, states that happiness often refers to the experience of joy, contentment, or positive well-being, combined with a sense that one's life is good, meaningful, and worthwhile (p. 52).

Positive psychologists initially concluded that we have a genetic set point for happiness that accounts for approximately 50 percent of how we generally feel. Our circumstances

(e.g., income, home, the climate we live in, etc.) appear to only account for about 10 percent of our total happiness. Fortunately, that leaves an additional 40 percent of happiness that is totally within our control via attitudes and choices. However, it is widely accepted that satisfaction is dynamic, and we do not make broad and general statements regarding substantial percentages. The causes of well-being can better be understood as a pie chart of influencers rather than fixed percentages (Peterson 2013).

There are many myths when it comes to determining the optimal pathway to experience a happier state. Many of us believe, "If I only had (you fill in the blank), I would be more satisfied. If I could change my circumstances (e.g., job, home, car, etc.), I would be happier." And lastly, many of us believe that happiness is something you either have or do not have.

The truth is that we tend to adapt to our circumstances, both good and bad, quickly. Indeed, you will likely be happier if you are blessed with good genes and optimal conditions. Fortunately, we do have some control over our feelings of happiness attributed to the attitudes and behaviors we choose each day.

There is a science of happiness that relates to recent findings in the human brain. You can train your brain to become happier. A more "positive brain" is linked to every domain of your life. As Richard Hanson, Ph.D., stated in his seminal book entitled *Hardwiring Happiness* (2013), all mental activity—sights and sounds, thoughts and feelings, conscious and unconscious processes—is based on underlying neural activity. Much mental and, therefore, neural activity flows through the brain like ripples on a river, with no lasting effects on its channel. But intense, prolonged, or repeated mental/neural activity—especially if it is conscious—will leave an enduring imprint in neural structure, like a surging current reshaping a riverbed. As they say in neuroscience: Neurons that fire together wire together.

Mental states become neural traits. Day after day, your mind is building your brain (p. 10). However, you can develop a positive mindset by savoring the good times longer with additional focused attention to become more aware of your mental processes without choosing via autopilot habitual choices and ingrained habits (Peterson 2013; Siegel 2011). For instance, what do you think about when taking a shower? Having warm water and feeling clean can be a positive contributor to your overall sense of well-being, but only if you intentionally try to be mindful and enjoy the experience. Taking a shower and ruminating about your seemingly endless to-do list is probably not as satisfying.

Being more aware of the present with greater clarity helps explore our inner lives, promoting more intentional and need-fulfilling choices and resulting from activities based on what is needed at any given moment. This keen awareness can significantly improve almost every aspect of your life, mainly if you can focus on the now of your experience. Savoring the present moment contributes to your well-being.

It necessitates sharing positive experiences with others, immersing yourself in an activity, and diverting yourself when you try to dampen a pleasant experience with unwanted self-statements and thoughts.

To illustrate the power of the mind, Dr. Jonathan Haidt, a professor at the University of Virginia, asked 350 students to engage in four activities in his introductory psychology class. One of the events was to indulge the senses by taking a break for ice cream in the middle of the afternoon and then savoring the ice cream.

This activity was enjoyable, but like all pleasures, it faded quickly. The other three activities were potentially gratifications: attend a lecture or class that you don't usually go to, perform an act of kindness for a friend who could use some cheering up, and write down the reasons you are grateful to someone and later call or visit that person to express your gratitude. Dr. Haidt's most significant findings were that people experienced longer-lasting improvements in mood from kindness and gratitude activities. Many students stated their good feelings continued the next day—which no one said about eating the ice cream (Haidt 2006).

Seeking pleasure is very tempting; satisfaction sometimes can be obtained via healthy behaviors such as a back rub or enjoying a warm breeze. However, gratifications often come from using one's strengths to accomplish, learn, and improve something meaningful. Kind acts are more enduring and often jump-start other influential and philanthropic endeavors.

Ironically, there is little relationship between money and materialistic items and sustained positive feelings. As Dr. David Meyers articulates in his book *The Pursuit of Happiness*, "Money is two steps removed from happiness: Actual in-
come doesn't much influence happiness; how satisfied we are with our income does. If we are content with how much it is, we are likely to say we are happy" (1992, p. 39). However, wealthy people take less pleasure in the small things in life, perhaps because they already have big things. Why don't all these extra gadgets and comforts make us significantly happier? Maybe it is because our behaviors and thoughts directly impact our feelings and physiology (Anchor 2013).

Some of our most satisfying experiences likely entail interacting with those whom we respect and admire. In an optimal environment, we seem to want to make choices that enhance our sense of sig-
nificance and feelings of self-worth. We also seem to need the freedom to control our lives and make choic-

es without coercion, threats, or bribery from others or the external world. We require fun and enjoyment. Throughout life, we need to experience enjoyable leisure pursuits.

Seemingly, happiness is a profound choice sustained by satisfying needs healthily and consistently, often regardless of external circumstances (Ricard 2003). Victor Frankl, an Austrian psychiatrist as well as a Holocaust survivor, stated: "What man needs is not a tensionless state, but rather the striving and struggling for some goal worthy of him. What he needs is not the discharge of tension at any cost, but the call of a potential meaning waiting to be fulfilled by him" (Ben-Shahar 2007).

According to many research studies, the number-one condition that trumps all others to predict happiness is satisfying relationships. Conversely, annoying and conflictual relationships are one of the surest ways to reduce your satisfaction. The best ingredients for improved relationships are good character, including trust, integrity, honesty, respect, responsibility, fairness, and altruism. That is why character will always matter as you pursue a fulfilling and happy life (Anchor 2013). Gratitude is an effective way to experience sustained happiness and well-being. Seemingly, happiness is reinforced by using your gifts to seize opportunities to bring out the best in others and make our world a better place. What activities lead you to sustained joy, contentment, and higher purpose in life?

Chapter 3

Developing a Capacity for Delight

When are you most likely to feel a sense of inner peace? The new wave in psychology that appears to cultivate inner peace is the practice of mindfulness. This entails finding a mental state where you can engage, let go of unhealthy thoughts, and accept whatever emotions you encounter. You can invite even negative emotions into the present and learn to let them go, just like a leaf falling into a stream. You can concurrently expand your awareness and open your senses to engage in the present.

Furthermore, you can clarify and live in harmony with your most essential values, such as love, peace, hope, respect, and compassion. Richard Hanson (2013) stated, "Staying mindful entails staying with the present moment by moment. Mindfulness itself only witnesses, but alongside that witnessing could be active, goal-directed efforts to nudge your mind one way or another" (p. 8). Practicing mindfulness can help you let go of the past and future and allow yourself to be fully present in the moment. Not only can this help with stress and anxiety, but it can also make your life so much more meaningful.

How often throughout the day do you notice what you are experiencing in the present? What are you seeing, hearing, and smelling, and how are you feeling? Horace Mann once stated, "Yesterday, somewhere between sunrise and sunset, two golden hours, each set with sixty diamond minutes. No reward is offered, for they are gone forever." This quote serves as a reminder of the importance of becoming still and enjoying the outdoors' beauty, a smile on someone's face, a warm shower, or the taste of a wonderful meal.

We want to be goal-directed but not governed. That is, we often borrow problems from the future when we lust for things and worry about what might happen. Peterson (2013) reviewed data from an extensive survey regarding how most people spent their day. The most frequent activities included "sleeping; working; doing household chores; eating and drinking; caring for others; engaging in leisure pursuits or sports and providing service through formal organizations" (p. 11). The miscellaneous or other category revealed an inordinate time spent shopping, talking on the phone, grooming, and dealing with email. Our biggest nemesis is often impatience. What is the point of saving time if we do not use it to savor what makes life compelling?

The lack of time can set the foundation for something that will make us feel better right now! Material items can be purchased as we are bombarded with advertisements that can trigger emotional desires—many of these items are perceived as being bet-ter than what we currently own. For instance, new cellular phones, computers, tablets, vehicles, and homes have improved features. We always seem to have to rejuice the juice of joy. Can you imagine having a black-and-white television with three channels and no remote control?

If you keep resting your mind on self-criticism, worries, grumbling about others, hurts, and stress, then your brain will be shaped into higher reactivity, vulnerability to anxiety and depressed mood, a narrow focus on threats and losses, and inclinations toward anger, sadness, and guilt (Hanson 2013, 11).

Fear is a part of life. The paradox is that triumph through fear breeds confidence, combined with rejoicing with your current successes and how far you have come in your life's journey. The psychologically rich, indeed, tend to become richer!

However, there are millions of individuals that continue to struggle with overwhelming feelings of anxiety. The symptoms tend to manifest in the following ways. Panic disorders include increased arousal, hyperventilation, dizziness, and often nausea. Generalized anxiety is a sense of worry or dread that lasts at least six months and robs one of pleasure. Social phobias are usually associated with individuals that avoid settings and activities that cause a person to blush, shake, or even sweat. Anxiety disorders can lead to exhaustion and often swirls with a mixture of depression. Small irritations can often feel like severe problems (Wehrenberg 2008).

Anxiety often has multiple causes linked to a genetic propensity for being hypersensitive, exaggerating the seriousness of real-life events, and then avoiding what may scare you the most. Avoidance ironically brings about more distress, worry, and rumination. The good news is that even though feeling anxious is not pleasant, it can be modified to an optimal level that makes you feel more passionate and energetic. To accomplish this, you must learn to control your brain chemistry (Anchor 2013).

Your brain consists of soft nervous tissue in vertebrates' skull, functioning as the coordinating center of sensation and intellectual and nervous activity. There are many great functions, including a complicated maze of 10 billion neurons, connecting with 10,000 other neurons. Wow, your cells and the complex network is almost infinite. Recent research with incredible technology has helped better understand the brain's ability to change throughout your lifetime. The term is often referred to as plasticity that means neurons that fire together wire together. The complex interconnection of neurotransmitters such as dopamine, serotonin, glutamate, gamma-aminobutyric acid (i.e., GABA), and norepinephrine have the most impact on feelings of anxiety. Your sympathetic nervous system can produce too much stress when your hypothalamus sends messages to your adrenal glands to release adrenaline and cortisol that are needed to release stores of energizing fuel such as glucose and fat that helps your muscles work hard. Bursts of energy can be helpful, but only when you need to act quickly to outwit something dangerous.

The area behind your forehead is part of the cerebral cortex's frontal lobe, the brain's most outermost section. This region is critical when you make choices regarding complex thinking and planning. Unfortunately, it is also the part of the brain that can suffer underdevel-

opment or damage with chronic distress or trauma. This is simplistic, but healthier choices—including reading, learning a musical instrument, or even participating in sports—can allow the brain to develop more emotional control, empathy, insight, and moral awareness. It is likely that individuals, and especially children, who endure detached and traumatic environments, have underdeveloped neural pathways.

Furthermore, stress hormones that are released too frequently can contaminate healthy neural pathways and connections. This likely leads to more emotional reactivity regulated by the fight-or-flight response initiated by the old brain and structures such as the amygdala (Siegel 2011). Some individuals have brains that are as finely tuned as race cars with no brakes. It is harder to stop and think about the right thing to do.

Many will, sadly, experience a horrific event in life. Feelings of being traumatized can ensue, which challenges the ability to cope effectively. A traumatic event impacts every aspect of your mind, body, and soul. Hypervigilance often follows as one tries to secure safety going forward. However, being on constant alert can be fatiguing. There is usually a feeling of helplessness and being overwhelmed, terrified of the future. Healthy coping strategies entail relearning to trust your senses, including vision, hearing, taste, smell, and touch, to become more balanced, integrated, and reassociated with feelings that you are indeed safe and secure.

If this sounds complicated, it is. Your body is prepared to protect itself from any real or perceived threat. Thinking is often too slow to respond to a traumatic event. You must react quickly and defend yourself.

Your old brain—often referred to as the periaqueductal gray region—gets lit up during a traumatic event and prepares you to be alert for any danger in the future in life. Areas of the brain responding to stress release cortisol and adrenaline, which directly impacts the brain. Cortisol can help control blood sugar levels, regulate metabolism, reduce inflammation, and assist with memory formulation. Cortisol will shut off the functioning of your hippocampus, and adrenaline will rev up the amygdala functioning. These two hormones have a vastly different impact on your total bodily response. Cortisol can be toxic to further brain development, and an abundance of adrenaline release increases the sensitivity to emotional memories. The fight, flight, and freeze responses are not always necessary and adaptive. Endorphins can be released when experiencing a horrific event that helps reduce the overall pain.

The three primary brain networks—the default mode network, the salience network, and the organizational system—can become impaired as there are so many potential threats in our environment.

The result is a contaminated ability to focus, plan, and make rational and practical decisions intended to solve problems. Disorganized detachment and feelings of disassociation are common and often become problematic. Approximately 20 percent of individuals that experience trauma will develop post-traumatic stress response. Memories too often become fragmented. Being frozen in time with a disturbing memory can erode feelings of well-being.

Being aware and present-focused helps to integrate energy and information flow. Responses then can become calmer and more rational, optimizing interactions with significant problem-solving, thus improving your daily habits. It is possible to change and heal your entire bodily functions.

Approximately 20 percent of individuals enduring an extraordinarily challenging and often horrific event develop post-traumatic stress disorder. The nervous system becomes unbalanced and tries to adjust to demands without recovery and rejuvenation. This blocks the capacity for flexible, adaptive, and stable healing. Brain functioning becomes disorganized, developing a need for greater integration, which refers to improve linkage to all parts of the body. Brain growth literally can become blocked when trauma is endured early in life. Vertical, left hemisphere, and right hemisphere brain functioning has difficulty with processing and integrating information. Emotional balance, rewarding relationships, and relaxation become exceedingly difficult. Thoughts, emotions, and your body cry out for security and safety and requires mindful awareness of everyday experience. Otherwise, past and scary memories can stimulate flashbacks and intrusive thoughts. The symptoms related to experiencing traumas can create much self-blame, such as, "Why am I so different and struggle so much, and why does fear paralyze me?" One can lose a sense of self.

Your stress response cannot be called into action regularly for a prolonged period without some sense of relief and rest. An optimal balance of neurochemical reactions is necessary as your brain monitors much of your functioning and impacts overall mood.  Each neurochemical has its specific role but affects your nervous system, stress response, limbic system, basal ganglia, and cortex. This is an oversimplification, but when there are minor imbalances in neurotransmitters, you can experience symptoms. Your hippocampus, which is part of the limbic register's details from your experience, sends them to your primary areas of executive functioning found in the cortex. The amygdala registers all emotions and almost serves like a smoke detector that goes off when it believes your need to survive a situation that is either real or just perceived as threatening.

Appropriate explanations of the brain would necessitate an entire book. Still, the primary goal in decreasing overwhelming feelings of anxiety is to have more control over the parasympathetic nervous system that can calm yourself down, breathe properly, relax, and refocusing to find a proper perspective, so your amygdala and hippocampus work together to differentiate what is dangerous and what is not. However, some techniques can quiet the part of your brain that tends to develop the "fight-or-flight" response (Wehrenberg 2008).

Ironically, real or perceived stress is not something you always want to fight or flee. Research indicates that even at high levels, adversity can often create more mental toughness, deeper relationships, heightened awareness, new perspectives, a sense of mastery, and a greater appreciation of life and the blessings you do have. However, these benefits necessitate a positive mindset and require that you look at the situation from a different perspective. It may be comforting to you that our brains have evolved with a built-in negativity bias.

"While the bias emerged in harsh settings very different from our own, it continues to operate inside us today as we drive in traffic, head into a meeting, settle a sibling quarrel, try to diet, watch the news, juggle household, pay bills, or go on a date. Your brain has a hair-trigger readiness to go negative to help you survive" (Hanson 2013, 20).

The antidote to the physical feeling of being afraid is to be very careful that you do not intake too many stress-enhancing substances such as caffeine, alcohol, tobacco, sugar, and even excessive sweeteners that all can trigger feelings of panic. Minimizing demands related to communication can help as well. That is, try to categorize responding to phone calls, emails, and text messages instead of letting them alert your brain throughout the day. Taking breaks and finding low-stimulation environments such as going for a short walk can also have many benefits to get away from the noise of stressful situations. Even looking outside, or at a favorite picture, or walking down a hallway can produce some symptom relief.

One's cognitions can be a gift or a curse depending on the context. Psychologists often caution, do not believe everything you think! I would like you to close your eyes and think about everything that has gone well in the last twenty-four hours. Perhaps you can think about specific incidents or just think about all the things you are grateful for. Now I would like you to focus on everything that has gone wrong. This can include but not be limited to irritating interactions with others, disappointments at work, all the things you are not looking forward to in the future, and so on.

Were you able to differentiate the overall changes in your mood? The power of positivity cannot be overemphasized. Still, it also takes much discipline to be more servant with your constant stream of automatic thoughts,

shared beliefs, and deep conviction that perhaps somehow you are incompetent—or worse, unlovable.

Our minds have evolved to attract the negative, as that kept us hypervigilant about possible dangers so we could take appropriate action. However, many of those threats are not rational, as there are not likely too many human-eating animals in your backyard. The old brain and its many functions to ensure survival is alive and well.

Years of evolution have developed superhighways that can signal our frontal cortex to be on alert and perhaps create possible worst-case scenarios that are irrational and unlikely to happen. For instance, how many things that you worried about last year became a reality?

It is not an event that directly impacts our overall feelings, but rather our perception and belief about the event. It is not uncommon to hear the statement, "This is one of the worst days of my life." Is that true? Perhaps your flight was delayed, and then your cell phone lost its charge. I don't want to be self-righteous, but I can indeed find many things to complain about, including being tall and crammed into an airplane seat with the person in front of me reclining during takeoff regardless of instructions not to do so. Perhaps another perspective is that it is incredible to sit in a seat, albeit with limited leg space, and fly across the United States in five hours. I wonder what my ancestors living in the early 1800s would have given to trade in their covered wagon if they could do so. Perhaps they were more worried about being safe rather than feeling good about the day.

Your brain is amazingly complicated and compelling. New research discoveries with the aid of advanced technology have allowed experts to learn more about the brain's functioning in the last ten years than at any other time in history. Your mind is a remarkable instrument that can generate thoughts and behaviors related to love, respect, and kindness. Still, it also has the power to intensify feelings of hatred, criticism, contempt, and self-loathing. Many of us tend to embellish the negative in situations because it may better prepare us for failure. We pay a significant price of the chronic stress that comes with cognitive distortions, such as: "My future is bleak." "School is stupid." "I am ugly." "This is the worst thing that could happen to me." "I will never find someone I can trust." "My cell phone sucks." "I hate my job."

The good news is that research is being conducted and finding new information regarding our brain structure's tremendous plasticity. We continue to create new neural connections and pathways each day. The old brain, which some researchers refer to as the elephant or emotional part of the brain, has been modified throughout years of evolution. It seemingly reacts quickly to real or perceived threats and gets spooked easily. There are superhighways in your old brain that can signal a fight-or-flight response. The frontal cortex of the brain struggles to quiet these fears once the process is engaged. However, it is hard to calm the old mind with the new brain because our pathways are like many back roads; our neural pathways are still developing to effectively quiet our fight-or-flight response.

Changing your negative self-statements is challenging yet possible. The process entails catching yourself when your self-statements and beliefs become irrational and distorted. Once you identify your thoughts immediately before unwanted strong and negative emotions, you can develop a consistent method of evaluating whether these thoughts are accurate and valid. Sometimes, just changing your behaviors can help shift your thoughts' focus and reduce the tendency to ruminate and make reality worse than it is. Every choice, including your thoughts and actions, has a complicated neurochemical consequence in the brain that impacts nearly every bodily function. The data show that self-denigration, perceptions of hopelessness, and sustained negativity serve as toxic waste, often manifesting in excessive depression and anxiety. Life becomes arduous, and each day may feel like total drudgery. Unfortunately, your mind can go to the negative to protect you from the worst-case scenario. You will likely pay the price for being hypervigilant to potential dangers that are improbable of really happening. The ability to expand your positivity by evaluating the validity of your thinking and perceptions can be instrumental in improving your psychological health and well-being. If that is too difficult, change your focus on the present and be mindful of a beautiful sunset, the feeling of a cool breeze on a hot day, or the smell of a tree or flower.

Life often brings challenges that one cannot minimize or deny. Tragic events such as being assaulted, suffering from a traumatic natural disaster, or even losing a loved one can be too emotionally painful. The myriad of strong emotions, in this case, necessitates dealing with fear and pain proactively as there appears to be a natural grieving process that facilitates emotional healing. Trying to outrun or deny these powerful feelings when life events are unfortunate creates a host of other problems that might manifest in different undesirable ways, such as suppressing your immune system making you more susceptible to emotional or physical issues.

The mind and body connection are intimate, and seeking help via the supportive nature of others, including professional counseling, must be viewed as a sign of courage rather than a weakness. Feelings of anxiety and panic are unpleasant and sometimes appear overwhelming. The real enemy is not your perception but the choice to avoid these feelings (Forsyth and Eifert 2007). The paradox is that the more we try to avoid painful emotions, the more intense they become. Also, you do not need to be sick to get better.

Professional and licensed mental health providers

often implement a process that encourages you to write down things you think whenever your emotions become intense. Your feelings are explored, and you can begin to practice a myriad of techniques to calm yourself and soften negative emotions. Deep breathing and learning to focus on your present sensations can start to slow your mind down so you can begin to think differently. Your feelings become your friend, which allows you to adjust your thinking and behaviors. Sadly, too many individuals turn to their default ways of being and often just try to grind their way through the day. The result is often physical, emotional, and even spiritual exhaustion. Short-term mood hits, such as alcohol and drugs, become more appealing but provide only temporary relief and deliver long-term negative consequences.

In our society, we too often view being busy as the antidote to not feeling well. Ironically, when you slow down, thoughts are stirred up regarding not being productive, which drives us to do more. Being relaxed and peaceful is a very functional state. Being overly busy and stressed-out is exhausting and distances us from our creativity and more profound wisdom, which helps us perform better. Relaxation is a highly productive state (Lake 2013, 210).

Learning to relax and calm oneself is relatively easy and natural. It typically necessitates focus on deep breathing and then being mindful of what your senses are experiencing. Attention on what you are seeing, hearing, smelling, and feeling focuses the mind and leads to more peaceful feelings. You can then be more aware of where your mind tends to drift and refocus with practice. Positive imagery that includes pleasant memories, experiences, and favorite places can also elicit almost immediate positive feelings that experience more inner peace. That is why meditation, mindfulness, prayer, visual imagery, biofeedback, or activities like yoga and tai chi are powerful antidotes to anxiety. The biggest challenge is often having the self-discipline to consistently give yourself breaks throughout the day to engage in more mindful methods.

Your feelings of positivity are fueled not only by realizing that you are capable and intelligent but also by effort and a positive mindset. A positive attitude is like an "I can do it" mentality. Optimism emanates from viewing potential problems as challenges looking for solutions and trumping negativity and pessimism by cultivating a sense of self-efficacy. Fortunately, you can train your mind to have a growth mindset that continually looks for solutions. In contrast, a negative mindset and resulting locked beliefs are the breeding ground for self-statements that often begin with "I can't..." Sadly, many begin to believe the following:

"I can't do math."

"I have always hated science."

"I wish I were smart enough to play a musical instrument."

"I should have learned a foreign language when I was younger because now, I am too old."

"I can never lose weight."

"I was not made to be physically active."

"There is no other type of work that I am good at."

"I just can't help myself."

"I am ugly."

"I will never discover a loving relationship."

"Something is very wrong with me."

I do not want to convey that you can easily change all your self-statements and core beliefs, but just review your life and remember the times you have overcome adversity or bounced back from failure. My guess is it likely entailed more of a growth mindset coupled with effort. Another advantage of developing a growth mindset is that it allows you to enjoy what you are doing. "Wow, I worked out for thirty minutes." You will likely look for other challenges. "I am a little sore, but I feel good about myself." You are not likely to be good at something without sustained effort. However, try to shrink change to develop optimism to set yourself up to have a good day.

There are so many possibilities to enrich your life. "This week, I am going to…"

Go for a walk.

Sign up for a photography class.

Reconnect with an old friend.
Hit golf balls on the range.
Learn to fly-fish.
Plan a vacation.
Go for a bike ride.
Learn how to play Pickleball.
Get a massage.
Engage in journaling, drawing, or painting.
Spend time in nature.
Attend a church service.

Ironically, you cannot help but change. Is the change intentional or just a result of trying to get through the day? A growth mindset is a belief that can be cultivated and is dynamic; it entails that change is always possible, and so much of it is in your control (Dweck 2007). Your mind, body, and soul, like everything else in life, needs time to recover. Prayer, meditation, yoga, listening to music, journaling, creative drawing, and usually spending time outside are helpful, especially when combined with deep breathing and a focus on your senses. This automatically calms the mind down and makes rumination and worry more challenging. Nutritious food and physical activity will further provide positive energy and resilience to handle the rigors of each day (Anchor 2013; Wehrenberg 2008).

Chapter 4

Nourishing Important Relationships

Who do you rely upon for encouragement and support? The best predictor of happiness is having enriched relationships and effectively meeting the need for love and belonging. With over 7.7 billion people in the world, developing social support and significant relationships would seemingly be easy. Ironically, just look at all the lonely people Although we have intuitively known that feeling loved and developing a sense of belonging and significance are primary needs, the data are clear and valid. The number-one predictor of happiness is social support. However, in a cluttered world, with so many individuals becoming a walking to-do list with emails stalking them, it seems more challenging to give other people time, attention, and affection. Technology is terrific, but digital signals are often a form of detached intimacy. They can never replace a deep and meaningful face-to-face interaction. Our cell phones appear to get much attention, but hopefully, they will never replace loving relationships.

Our need for social support, love, and belonging is rooted deeply in our genetic makeup. When we make positive social connections, pleasure-inducing hormones such as oxytocin are released into the brain and help us feel better and improve concentration and focus while serving as a buffer against anxiety and depression. Strong social support, including being married, has many protective factors that create a strong emotional and physical resilience and help us live longer and increase the quality of our lives (Anchor 2013).

We now know from research that significant relationships and marriages need nourishment in a positive climate of respect and affection (Gottman 2011). Feelings of sadness, discouragement, disappointment, frustration, and anger naturally flow from daily life experiences. Although negativity is inevitable and even productive, it also increases awareness of what is not working and may prevent your relationship's erosion that typically follows this path:

*You meet, and there is a strong attraction.

*Feelings of happiness are with anxiety about whether this person wants to stay in your life.

*The attraction is mutual and sustained, and you may become married.

*Inevitable problems in marriage occur as your lives become more hectic and busier.

*You do not manage conflicts respectfully and proactively.

*Resentment accrues, and disputes escalate to

a point where you no longer feel like you are on the same team.

*You begin to withdraw and forget about the facilitating forces that were supposed to bind you together for life.

*You begin to associate your partner with negative feelings and protect your sense of self by using criticism, blame, and threats.

*You withdraw from your partner and try to stay unhappily married or expedite a break from the negativity through a divorce.

*You try to heal from the intense pain and feelings of shame related to the loss of the vision for a wonderful, lifelong relationship with the person you once loved (Markman, Stanley, and Blumberg 2011).

Marriage is not a panacea for all our social ills, yet in most cases, it produces many positive consequences and overall is good for society. Intact and healthy marriages serve as a gift to promote child and family development that extend across race, ethnicity, and class lines. Policymakers interested in decreasing poverty and crime while concurrently increasing child well-being and raising economic status would benefit by developing community initiatives and programs to strengthen marriage.

What destroys a marriage? Is it a terrible sex life, extended families, finances, health problems, poor communication, too few leisure outlets? Marriages are quite resilient; however, negativity has the highest potential to contaminate slowly and ultimately destroy a marital relationship. The worst culprits include but are not limited to conveying that your partner is the problem because of some defect in personality sent via criticism. This is quite a different behavior when compared to complaining about the response. A complaint frequently begins with "you always" or "you never."

Criticism is often followed by becoming defensive. This behavior typically manifests in counter-complaining or acting like an innocent victim. Accepting responsibility for a complaint is often a helpful antidote to soften emotional reactivity.

Disrespect and contempt are the most devastating and best predictors of divorce. Disrespect and contempt often involve sarcasm, mocking, hostility; calling your partner a derogatory name is an obvious recipe for disaster. Partners that have successful marriages are much more appreciative of their partners. Encouragement and praise are crucial.

Stonewalling is a form of emotional withdrawal that further contaminates loving feelings in marriage. This happens when listeners distance themselves from a conversation, offering no physical or verbal cues after being affected by what they hear. Ironically, acting like you do not care is typically accompanied by a rapid heart rate and blood pressure, negatively impacting your immune system. Being attentive and turning toward your partner is crucial to resolving your relationship (Gottman 2011).

Imagine living with your best friend for the next 15,000 days—even the healthiest and most compelling friendship is full of challenges. Welcome to married life. Living your life with someone you love is more appealing than living life alone, regardless of the moments of adversity and stress. Marriage is an opportunity to share your experience, dreams, and aspirations with someone you love who brings out the best in you. Marriage is one of the few life choices that will truly transform your present and future. Ironically, we live in a society that emphasizes the wedding day rather than preparation for this lifetime commitment and change.

What would it be like to be in a significant relationship with you? Undoubtedly, it is complicated to predict what the rest of your lives together will be like, especially as you both will encounter so many life experiences and transitions. How do you know that you are compatible with living the rest of your life with someone you think you love? We all have our relational strengths and growth areas. However, many individuals tend to be flaw-finders rather than talent scouts. Conversely, happily married couples behave like good friends and handle their conflicts in gentle, positive ways. You should consistently seize opportunities to bring out the best in your partner.

Chapter 5

Moving Toward Wellness

Wellness is a holistic philosophy of life that includes promoting positive health by improving one's quality of life, thus elevating happiness and well-being. It is an active process of becoming aware of and making choices toward a better existence. Perhaps the helpful question is to ask, "Why don't I feel well?" There is no perfect prescription for wellness, but there are so many facilitating forces. Listening to your body is a wonderful yet often scary way to begin. Your goal is to find the best course of going forward.

Wellness is a journey that begins within you. Incorporating a wellness lifestyle is a lifelong adventure rather than a short-term all-or-nothing attitude boot camp. We have all lived  through unhealthy times in this life, and our bodies have cried out for detoxification. Applying a healthy lifestyle can be intimidating, but there are protocols to be well that you can tailor to your unique orientation to life (Lapine 2017).

Consider giving yourself the freedom to modify your life. Overall, wellness improvement can appear daunting. Change can be challenging. However, you can increase the likelihood you can transform your life by making small habit changes. You will not become the healthiest person on the planet, and your more beneficial endeavors do not need to become a competition. Water, sleep, and physical activity may be a wonderful place to start. You may also do an inventory of your vices you want to change the most such as alcohol, sugar, and caffeine. Developing a new path forward can inspire you to interrupt old unhealthy patterns and focus on small changes that can begin a slow but powerful transformation.

Stress will be a part of our lives for as long as we live. The critical factor becomes how we can manage it. Pressure can be positive unless it exceeds one's capacity to cope. We need a certain amount of stress in our lives to not only survive but also to thrive. It is challenging to learn how to invite the optimal level of stress into our lives to help experience higher wellness and well-being levels. This is accomplished by learning to develop a positive attitude, putting problems in perspective, learning to relax, eating healthily, being physically active, obtaining enough deep sleep, and living in a place that evokes relaxed feelings. These facilitating forces become the feel for your wellness journey.

Physical activity is an opportunity to disengage from the grind of everyday living and work and helps you to relax, reflect, and think creatively. There appears to be ample evidence that physical activity not only reduces the likelihood of illness and disease but also promotes more energy and mood elevation.  "People who exercise at least two days a week are happier and have significantly less stress" (Fredrickson 2009, 78). Exercise physiologists are now advocating that we take as many opportunities to become active throughout each day as possible. Excellent physiological and psychological benefits can be derived from accumulating activity throughout the day. Safe activities such as walking can significantly benefit your overall health and wellness. Cardiovascular strength and efficiency can be accomplished via endurance activities such as swimming, biking, and jogging. Proper stretching can facilitate flexibility, while resistance training is vital to strengthen muscles. All these activities will help refuel your energy system.

Nutritional awareness is a complex young science

that entails much speculation and confusion. However, learning where food comes from its composition and its effect is instructive. Too often, the focus is on dieting rather than eating healthily. We all know what we should be eating. Fruit, vegetables, and lean meats are usually about 10 percent of what is sold at the grocery store and probably would not generate any profit without the many processed foods high in fat, sugar, and salt. You and I also know that we should drink plenty of water and be physically active for at least thirty minutes a day.

Most of us have been informed that there is no quick fix, and loss of body fat necessitates eating a balanced, portion-controlled intake of daily calories coupled with increasing our activity level. Healthy nutrition does necessitate self-discipline. Wellness is a lifetime endeavor, and to experience its benefits, one must learn to enjoy the process. Most nutritional experts agree that eating a variety of foods, including balancing calories with physical activity and encouraging yourself to consume more healthy foods like vegetables, fruits, whole grains, fat-free and low-fat dairy products, and seafood, and consuming less sodium, saturated and trans fats, added sugars, and refined grains need to become a lifetime habit. Our lapses that may include binging on greasy burgers,

French fries, malts, potato chips, and doughnuts must become less frequent, and our overall wellness will be compromised. We know that even foods with empty calories can be consumed with moderation. However, how many of us eat these things in moderation?

To overcome the temptation, seek the support of significant others who can encourage healthy eating patterns and perhaps track your intake of foods and water. Also, be aware of old cues, which have been conditioned with poor eating habits, such as the reclining chair in the living room. Eat smaller portion sizes and concentrate on savoring the taste, texture, and aroma of your food. Give your fork and spoon a more extended rest between bites. Put down the newspaper and turn off the television and cell phone. Drinking more water and getting rid of empty calories at home will likely help as well. Too often, overeating is related to an emotional state. We tend to blow it when we have feelings of boredom or are nervous, sad, or depressed. Unfortunately, unhealthy foods become emotionally nurturing and provide a perceived temporary lift. This mood-altering fix lasts a short time and typically leads to more cravings and feelings of guilt and shame. Attempts to reduce these feelings can include self-statements such as, "I'll wait until Monday to start eating better," or "What difference does it make now? I have already blown it." It is crucial to deal with our emotional states instead of looking for a short-term psychological lift. This is difficult but possible when you conclude that great-tasting, high-calorie foods will not help you resolve your emotionally laden issues. A wellness lifestyle can help confront problems proactively.

Your quest for greater wellness is facilitated by finding the right blend of healthy eating, accumulation of movement throughout the day, and quality sleep. Although challenging, it is possible, but when sustained, the intersection of these endeavors will improve your daily energy, mood, and the probability of living a longer, healthier life (Rath 2013).

Creating a culture of healthy living necessitates being more vigilant about every choice and consequence. How can you fill your home with more nutritious foods, create an environment that ensures longer and deeper sleep, and get at least thirty to sixty minutes of physical activity a day? Useful tips include just making small changes or shifts to your lifestyle. Remind yourself that small changes can lead to a transformation. Consistently engaging in a healthy habit for thirty days can lead to a lifelong endeavor.

The US Department of Health and Human Services and US Department of Agriculture recommends the following guidelines for healthy nutritional goals: It has been said that our bodies are our gardens, to which our wills are our gardeners. Dietary Guidelines for Americans emphasize that all food and beverage choices matter. Healthy eating patterns help maintain healthy body weight, promote nutrient adequacy, and reduce chronic disease risk. Choosing nutrient-dense foods is essential to nourish your mind, body, and soul.

Additional tips for healthy eating entail understanding the following:

*Morning activity is optimal as it leads to a cascade of healthier choices throughout the day.

*Fad diets are the recipe for failure.

*Remind yourself that inactivity is a depressant.

*You are ironically more productive long-term when you get more sleep.

*Every bite you take of food either is a net gain or loss (e.g., vegetables vs. French fries; water vs. soda).

*There will be likely healthy and unhealthy ingredients in many meals, but if you were an accountant, which would be a net gain or loss to your overall health and energy for living?

*Sitting may be deemed hazardous to your long-term health.

*The quality of sleep can have a significant contribution to either having a good or bad nutritional day.

*Too much sugar is a toxic waste to your body and likely is associated with diabetes, obesity, heart disease, and perhaps cancer.

*Foods with sugar will become addictive, as it will create a short-term emotional high, followed by craving, and creates a subtle addiction with long-term detrimental effects.

*Walking and stretching throughout the day helps your overall energy level.

*You can usually judge food quality by its color (fruits and vegetables with vibrant colors are almost sure to be right for you).

*Measuring the steps you take during the day may be helpful, and if you can average 5,000 to 10,000 steps a day, you will feel so much better.

*Refined and processed foods are probably at the center of the obesity universe.

*Family-style serving probably leads to enormous portion sizes of food.

*I know this is exceedingly difficult, but eating nuts, seeds, apples, celery, and carrots instead of crackers and chips and snack bars would help you lose body fat and boost your mood.

*You already realize that you are more likely to make poor choices when you are hungry.

*Artificial blue light will likely impact your melatonin levels and erode your quality of sleep (Rath 2013).

Most of us make better choices without the judgment or criticism of others. Cultivating the discipline to want to feel better and more energetic is a worthy pursuit rather than solely focusing on weighing less. We all need to make our own choices without unreasonable external demands from others. Some individuals view the world as possibilities and have a fantastic ability to use their freedom of choice. They do not allow someone else to deter their hopes and dreams. Although life is not fair, and there are many facilitating and detracting forces that influence our choices, we must ultimately seize the freedom to choose our attitudes and behaviors intimately linked to how we feel. Freedom is often discovered not by avoiding bad feelings but by confronting them. Feelings of unworthiness and alienation can thwart our essential goodness and inherent tendency to thrive in life.

Unhealthy compensation for feelings of inferiority sets the stage for poor choices that provide a short-term respite from suffering but lead to long-term negative consequences and possible dependence on alcohol, drugs, shopping, sexualized behavior, overeating, and even perhaps grueling work—an addiction that our society too often applauds. Numerous self-improvement projects are sold with false promises of magically eradicating our problems. However, they are often illusions that allow you to play it safe rather than risk confronting challenging feelings and the ultimate fear of failure. Attempts to cope and just try to survive the day take us away from fully experiencing the present moment as feelings of worry, dread, and free-floating anxiety lurking everywhere we turn often lead to exhaustion and depression. We somehow believe we can outrun these negative emotions by keeping busy, becoming our own worst critic, or developing a keen sense for other people's flaws.

It is perfectly normal to have negative emotions, and it is impossible to pretend they do not exist. It is possible to view unpleasant feelings as a warning sign that alerts you to make healthier choices. You can allow these feelings to flow in and out through deep breathing, physical activity, prayer, meditation, or any other way to experience and then let go of fear, insecurity, and anger. Emotional states are dynamic and will change with proper focus. Try to catch your negative self-statements and rumination about "if only or what if" worst-case possibilities and then divert and modify your behaviors and remind yourself of the things you are grateful for daily. You can also nourish your body, mind, and soul with healthy nutrition throughout an entire day. Try to focus on the positive aspects of your life and what is truly going right will lift your mood. Also, opportunities to help others is not only a wonderful gift to them but also yourself. It has numerous mental health benefits that can positively affect your life.

It is sad when bad things happen to good people. However, just as in past generations, we must keep hope alive and realize that almost all adversity can be overcome with a more productive attitude, perspective, and focus on what you can control. Lastly, ensuring healthy relationships with family, friends, and community is life's most significant predictor of happiness and sustained joy.

Stress in life is a good thing, as it motivates us to accomplish meaningful tasks. However, when it appears that terrible events exceed our capacity to cope, distress can take its toll on one's emotional, physical, and spiritual well-being.

The byproduct of distress can be feeling demoralized, hopeless, cynical, and angry. These negative feelings are exacerbated if one has difficulty changing to a more positive mindset that broadens one's perspective.

The key to building your tolerance for stress and bounce back from adversity, trauma, and threats to one's livelihood are called resilience. This is a choice, but it is easier for some, especially when they cope healthily. In an excellent book entitled *Resilience: The Science of Mastering Life's Greatest Challenges*, Steven M. Southwick, MD, and Dennis S. Charney, MD, advocate the following practical advice for becoming more optimistic, which is the fuel for overcoming adversity and jump-starting positive energy to elicit resilience:

*Try to remember that difficulties do not last forever. Take one day at a time and do not borrow problems from the future that may not occur.

*Where there may now be pain, over time, good things will likely return.

*Keep the adverse event within limits; do not let it pervade other areas of your life (e.g., family relationships, etc.).

*Think of the strengths and resources you can use to help deal with the problem.

*Notice what is right; for example, acts of kindness and altruism are antidotes for stress, and it is better to give than receive.

*Rely on your religious or spiritual beliefs to gain a healthier perspective and give you the strength to face your fears.

*Try to do the right thing and dig deep to find the character strengths within you, even though it feels like there is a cost for you to pay.

*Please remember that social support is the most significant buffer of stress, and isolation is typically a recipe for psychological disaster.

Lastly, be reminded that you can control things, such as healthy eating and physical activity, and then recover and obtain restful sleep. You do not have to look at your situation from rose-colored glasses. However, please be reminded that almost all individuals who cope in healthy ways overcome adversity within a relatively short time. Pursuing the good life takes more than understanding and fantasizing about it.

The easiest way to change how you feel is to change thinking and actions. We can make human behavior too complicated, but regardless of what psychological theories propose, they all necessitate an ultimate focus on increasing the likelihood that you make the choices that produce desired consequences. Although issues such as free will can be debated, we seemingly all have many options today that are within our control. Consequently, ask yourself, "What are the opportunities for learning and growth today, and how can I be helpful to others?" (Dweck 2009). The key is, "Let other people matter" (Peterson 2013, 81).

Chapter 6

Finding Meaning in Work

Discovering a meaningful career is exciting, sometimes scary, and, quite frankly, a vast choice point in your life. I continue to be amazed at how many hours of life are consumed by work. Furthermore, I must confess that I worry about the new generation as they enter a hypercompetitive job market that seems to change each day. As a result, thriving in life requires a comprehensive self-evaluation of your interests, values, life experiences, passion, and competencies. You will likely need to tolerate ambiguity, as the days of stable careers with a thirty-year relationship with a company appear to be rare. Furthermore, not too many jobs entail obtaining a company car, country club membership, and more-than-adequate health benefits and pension.

Do you view your work as a job, career, or calling? Your answer has profound implications for your overall satisfaction. A high-paid banker who just cares about money and does not like the work will spend a lot of time being unhappy. A custodian in a low-income nursing home that views the work as a calling connects with the people they work with and enjoys helping others. Watering plants or straightening pictures is very meaningful when it brightens the life of someone else.

Career counseling is often challenging. I do not want to thwart dreams, yet there is a time when one must be realistic. For instance, many high school students may wish to become medical doctors, although they do not want to take advanced chemistry, biology, and physics and may not score well on their MCAT.

The job market will be changing at a staggering pace, and labor and manufacturing jobs diminish. It helps if your passion, strengths, and talents align with the evolution of new and expanding demand areas, such as technology and health care. Fully understanding what you want to do with the rest of your life is nearly impossible. Sometimes, future opportunities do not become apparent until you reach the age of mid-twenties and beyond. It is challenging to know what you want to do when you have not thoroughly used your skills in various areas.

However, it is possible to be headed the right direction toward a meaningful career.

What gets you most excited about your job or career going forward? Most of us just want to have a job, and then there may be a quest to become successful, and ultimately, you will likely ask yourself, "Does the work I do today matter?" My hope for you is that you find your work both exciting and meaningful. Furthermore, receiving a fair wage for what you do is also essential. However, the ultimate answer may be to reduce expenses and focus more on basic needs versus an infinite array of wants.

In the book *Die Empty: Unleash Your Best Work Every Day* (2013), the author, Todd Henry, cautions anyone seeking meaningful work to avoid the "seven sins of mediocrity." These entail:

*Aimlessness. Do not choose a career as if you were shooting a bow and arrow at a target blindfolded.

*Boredom. This is typically a sign that your mind has grown weary of not stretching your comfort zone.

*Comfort. The desire of seeking the easy way generally is the enemy of greatness.

*Delusion. Have a sense of your true gifts, talents, and competence.

*Ego. Are you resilient enough to handle failure and fall forward?

*Fear. Choices become scarier when you avoid the unknown.

*Guardedness. When you choose to cut yourself off from others and refuse to become vulnerable, it will be more challenging to see your gifts and talents (Henry 2013).

Career decisions and transitions are relevant. An optimal process would be first to align your work with what you value. Making choices aligned with your values may necessitate observing what you would want to be doing regardless of income. You also would benefit by obtaining brutally honest feedback regarding what you do well. Every job requires differing competencies. You may need to have other individuals give you helpful feedback related to the following questions:

*What is explicitly happening when I produce quality results?

*What am I doing when I am most enthusiastic?

*What work environment brings out the best in me?

*Do I prefer to be surrounded by colleagues or work more independently?

*Do I tend to need organization and stability?

*If it were not for pay, what would I enjoy doing?

*What am I engaged in when I lose track of time?

Career planning is an ongoing process that helps you continue learning, growing, and developing. The process typically entails the following: fully understanding your interests, values, skills, and preferences; exploring possibilities and opportunities that are available to you and fit well with your life circumstances; and continuing to clarify precisely what challenges you, what you enjoy, and what you excel in.

The process is dynamic and continues throughout your entire life. As a result, it helps to know yourself. Conduct research on numerous careers. Make choices that get you closer to what you want to do. Then take action to find a job that utilizes your strengths and talents in a world that is changing each day.

Enjoying what you do requires a positive outlook, which is also related to your ultimate success. Please be reminded that your IQ score is an invalid attempt to measure your intelligence, and it accounts for only 33 percent of overall success at work. Your intelligence must be augmented with three fundamental beliefs (Anchor 2013).

I began my career in psychology by administering numerous intelligence tests. The assessments were a reliable and valid measure of one's aptitude that were developed to predict the present and future academic and employment success. The estimates did seem to be a reasonably good measure of memory and problem-solving, now referred to as crystallized and fluid intelligence. However, something felt intuitively unjust about these assessments, which seemed to fail to measure the essential traits, knowledge, and skills needed to flourish in life. I now realize these assessments did not measure the test taker's social skills, emotional maturity, creativity, common sense, or character strength. I remember one question from an IQ test that asked a youngster, "Where does bacon come from?" He responded, "A grocery store." Unfortunately, the correct response was from a pig. His response and other reasonable answers decreased his overall intelligence score. Was this a valid question to measure intelligence? However, who was I to question these tools held in such high esteem by many prominent psychologists and educators?

Do you believe you are gifted intellectually? Thankfully, Dr. Howard Gardner, a highly esteemed trailblazer regarding giftedness, began to dispute equating intelligence with an IQ score from an assessment. His seminal research and developing theories about intelligence expanded the notion that your aptitude is so much more than an IQ score, which puts so much emphasis on one's ability to remember words and solve problems. Many domains exist in various cultures to help one reach essential goals. He believed there is a multitude of intelligence, entirely independent of each other; each intelligence has its strengths and constraints; that the mind is far from unencumbered at birth (Gardner 2011). No two individuals are the same. Not even identical twins possess a detailed profile of intelligence (Anchor 2013).

Becoming more intelligent is not necessarily the goal of education. Instead, the school serves as a facilitating force that allows us to develop higher character and competence, which leads to meaningful endeavors, including work. Dr. Gardner's main interest is to better value and measure interpersonal intelligence, which profoundly impacts how you work with a group of peers rather than how many answers you get correct on a multiple-choice examination. The future will likely add additional domains of intelligence that we believe exist yet are challenging to measure. Our intelligence knowledge will probably broaden soon (Gardner 2011).

If you were not placed in a gifted program, what intelligences do you utilize to produce quality results? For instance, do you have a sensitivity to spoken and written language referred to as linguistic intelligence? Can you quickly analyze problems analytically and enjoy math and science, traits related to possessing a high degree of logical-mathematical intelligence? Do you gravitate toward musical intelligence, where you have developed performance, composition, and appreciation of melodic patterns? Are you incredibly coordinated with your bodily movements and can use your mind and body to excel in sports, dance, and other activities that necessitate whole body movement? Do you readily recognize patterns of vast spaces and confined areas and easily find your way through mazes or read maps to provide the appropriate direction based on viewing the entire lay of the land, relying on your unique intelligence? Do people find you very approachable and tell you about their life challenges because of your interpersonal intelligence? They realize you can easily express your true self and are keenly perceptive, possess a high degree of empathy and compassion, and radiate positive energy to others, thus being encouraging. Can you easily self-evaluate and understand yourself and others, which gives you an intrapersonal ability to help regulate your life and others? Can you easily navigate your way through nature and the outdoors and easily recognizable features of the environment with your natural talents (Gardner 2011)?

There are additional intelligence types that exist, but they are too hard to measure accurately, such as spiritual or moral intelligence. Regardless, the good news is that you are gifted in a unique way. In certain cultures, the bad news is that some intelligence types are held in high esteem and may create an unfair bias in our educational and work environments. You can see why being an educator is challenging.

What type of work is essential to you? The first is believing that your behavior matters. If you believe a task is necessary, you are more focused and put forth more effort. You remember subjects or courses in school that just did not seem to have any practical  value to life. Your studies became more of a chore or job, with little satisfaction. It is not surprising that excellent educators and bosses explain the desired outcomes of learning new skills that broaden our vision and passion. Second, a positive support network with individuals who believe you can accomplish essential tasks is critical. Encouragement and optimism from others are contagious. The third crucial ingredient for success and satisfaction at work is how you perceive jobs. Do you typically view your career as a distressful threat or a significant challenge? Your work environment matters. Negative, and at times, malicious individuals are genuinely toxic, but you cannot control their behavior. However, you can control how you respond to them, or perhaps it is better to limit your interactions with them to a minimum. Negativity becomes like secondhand smoke in the workplace. Developing a positivity antidote may entail starting the day by writing down three things that you are grateful for at work.

Individuals who are saturated with problems are challenging but try to get them off the topic at hand. It is probably not wise to agree with their negativity or argue with them; find a subject that they might enjoy. There must be something going right in their lives, and then you can reinforce with positivity.

The following reminders may help you set yourself up each day to feel better.

*It is acceptable to be happy, kind, patient, relaxed, and forgiving.

*Becoming stuck in a rat race of life is a choice.

*It is not a badge of honor to work more hours than necessary to achieve quality results.

*Rest is not only acceptable but necessary and a healthy choice.

*You have a choice not to become frustrated.

*It feels good to go out of your way to be kind.

*A solution-oriented approach is so much more useful than excessive complaining about problems.

*Commiserating with others about the issues at work will likely make you feel more hopeless.

*Try not to gossip about others.

*Be reminded that every person wants to be appreciated and feel valued.

*Being respectful to others is simply the right thing to do and does not need an ulterior motive.

*Accept the fact that you have an occasional bad day.

*Your best ideas will probably come when you are relaxed and quiet your mind.

*Try to prioritize your daily activities.

*Examine your unhealthy rituals and habits and be willing to change them.

*Try to focus on the present moment and ask yourself, "Next year will I care about this problem?"

The job that makes you the happiest is likely when there is an intersection of what you are good at, something you find meaningful, and of course, something you enjoy. When you find a job that feels like a calling, it does not seem like work. Instead, you often find yourself in the flow, and time goes by quickly. You lose yourself in time and feel energized. Your brain's resources have a crystal-clear focus on what you are doing. It can be a tight zone to find, but very possible if you are appropriately challenged. You are also more likely to look forward to the next day (Anchor 2013).

Why do some people succeed at work while their colleagues, many of whom are intellectually gifted, do not do as well? Daniel Goleman, who has a Ph.D. from Harvard University, contends that only 25 percent of work performance can be attributed to sheer mental aptitude. In a world where job security in many places is tenuous at best, it seems vital to know how one can excel at work and seek stability and perhaps advancement. Academic or technical ability is quickly becoming the threshold required to enter a job. However, becoming a high performer necessitates resilience, initiative, optimism, adaptability to change, and empathy toward others. These attributes are often described as emotional intelligence and closely related to the possession of good character, that is, caring about how one's behavior impacts others.

Emotional intelligence is not just about being nice or expressing feelings. Instead, it builds upon one's knowledge and skills. It helps one become a primary leader of an organization by developing big-picture thinking, political awareness, confidence, and intuition (Goleman 2006).

Mindsight is coined by Dr. Dan Siegel to describe our human capacity to perceive the self and others' minds. It is a powerful lens through which we can understand our inner lives with more clarity, integrate the brain, and enhance our relationships with others. Mindsight is a kind of focused attention that allows us to see the internal workings of our minds. It helps us get ourselves off the autopilot of ingrained behaviors and habitual responses. It lets us "name and tame" the emotions we are experiencing, rather than being overwhelmed by them.

This becomes our seventh sense, which can contribute to our well-being. We can begin to make choices with our brain in mind that will provide a more abundant life by explor-  ing the subjective essence of who we are, create more profound meaning in life, and better regulate our emotional responses with a sense of balance and appropriateness given the stressors, both good and bad that we face (Siegel 2011).

More good news from the research front indicates that mindsight can be cultivated regardless of your earlier history through practical steps. This learned process can change your brain's physical structure according to new scientific discoveries in the last twenty years. We are not only growing new connections in our mind in childhood but literally throughout our entire life. This leads to better integration with the brain and helps us control our choices instead of just reacting in a similar fashion, which is often too emotional and sometimes even dangerous. This newfound freedom and flexibility are exhilarating. It is becoming more common for individuals like yourself to state, "My entire view of reality has changed toward the positive." Of course, developing mindsight takes effort, time, and practice. A fancy word that you will frequently hear in the future is neuroplasticity, which describes our ability to grow new neurons in response to new experiences.

Educators are often pressured to prepare curricula that rapidly change and improve your crystallized and fluid intelligence (e.g., memory and problem-solving). These are essential areas, and with the effort, you can likely learn many concepts that will help you become proficient in these areas. However, there are significant areas such as your character, creativity, ability to work with your hands, and interpersonal skills. So, you may be very gifted in something that can never be measured by a test. Although you may not reap enormous benefits in school, the workplace will reward these skills, especially if you find an environment and job description that appears to bring out the best in you. Intelligence and character are both critical. Societies run by smart people without a moral foundation can easily find ways to suppress, marginalize, and even hurt others.

It is challenging yet possible to develop the mindset that today is truly a gift and commit to happiness. All days are created equally, and your present moment is just as crucial as any future day. Success is increased when one is optimistic and seizes opportunities and challenges. Lastly, be reminded that it is true that individuals on their death bed are unlikely to wish they would have spent more time at work.

Chapter 7

Making Our World a Better Place

Our youth are our future. Pursuing the good life entails trying to provide every youngster with time, attention, and affection from parents and other caring adults, so they feel a sense of significance and belonging. It is difficult to thrive in life if there is not a healthy moral landscape. This appears to increase the ability to influence positive attitudes and behaviors from both children and adolescents. Spending quantity and quality time with the child promotes a healthy, emotional attachment and encourages learning essential life traits such as cooperation, self-esteem, courage, and responsibility.

I realize that older individuals too often look at the next generation being raised as a train wreck. Of course, there are legitimate concerns about the current well-being of our youth and the lack of physical activity, constant temptations to

overly focus on new advances with technology, and perhaps a growing sense of entitlement ("I want what I want, and I want it now"). However, they are expressing themselves to a world that we created for them. The good news is that technology has made our world smaller and more accessible to become more culturally literate.

We are blessed to have numerous parents and communities who tirelessly try to give their children what they need to thrive in life. Daily, innumerable educators, school counselors, and administrators are dedicating their entire professional careers to help students develop competence and good character, which build a foundation for lifelong learning and productive citizenship. Furthermore, we have numerous leaders whose lives are filled with integrity and moral courage. Yes, there are so many people in our community who try to make our world a better place and serve as an inspiration.

As Stephen Covey articulates so well in his 2006 book entitled Everyday Greatness, "The majority of people in this world are good people doing good things, and that we should not let the noise of the negative minority drown out the steady sound of good that is around us" (p. viii).

We all applaud the many isolated heroic acts of

courage, but the goodness that lives on comes from ordinary people doing extraordinary things even when there is a cost.

Every day we have an opportunity to make choices that promote helping us become trustworthy, respectful, responsible, fair, caring, and good citizens. Please be reminded that character will never go away if individuals are thinking, acting, and feeling. We can choose to be more intentional about teaching, advocating, and modeling good character or give in to a life full of cynicism that entails, "I can't make much of difference, and kids will be kids."

Stephen Covey challenges us all with three critical questions:

"Is your life like driftwood being tossed to and fro, or are you instead of making your waves and going in a direction you—by choice—want to go?

"To what ends, or purposes, are your daily choices leading? To what ends, or purposes, would you like them to lead?

"Is your life in harmony with timeless, universal principals?" (Covey 2006, xv).

Spending meaningful time with children, coupled with encouraging them to play, is a powerful combination, but perhaps becoming more challenging because of work demands and growing materialistic needs. Children and adolescents typically have exceptional energy levels. Unstructured play, especially in the younger years, is invaluable and allows children to learn and renew by being active, creative, and spontaneous. The increase in energy appears to help them become more focused on daily tasks and responsibilities such as schoolwork. The play also helps kids learn positive peer relationships, reduces stress and tension, promotes brain development, and serves as a healthy activity that often aids physical activity and wellness

How can you interact with a child in a meaningful way? Too many children are being lured into sedentary lifestyles by being overly exposed to television, computer time, and video games. These activities seem to raise the threshold necessary for kids to experience long-term joy and happiness. Youth are being bombarded by provocative images including, but not limited to, violence, sex, and bizarre lifestyles, which just seem to change brain chemistry to want more. This feel-good treadmill never seems to end in any type of enduring satisfaction and fulfillment. Furthermore, it often leads to youngsters becoming less sensitive to others' pain and suffering, more fearful, or more aggressive (Meyers 2000).

Richard Louv, in his seminal book entitled *Last Child in the Woods*, stated that there is a growing body of research that links our mental, physical, and spiritual health directly to our association with nature. Spending time in nature opens our senses to the richness of the human experience. His book sparked the children-in-nature movement and builds a case that the health of children and the health of the earth are inseparable. The message galvanized a back-to-nature campaign that hopes to reduce childhood obesity, attention disorders, and depression.

It is easy to feel guilty for giving kids your leftover energy. Well-intended yet guilt-ridden, parents so desperately want their kids to be happy that they often try to please their kids by being permissive or giving them an abundance of material things.

Furthermore, spoiling kids with stuff reinforces entitlement and the wanting more. This sense of entitlement becomes very frustrating to parents who have worked hard for what they have. It also erodes proper character development (Britzman and Hanson 2005).

As children enter adolescent years, hopefully, the stage has been set for them to become more responsible, dedicated, and involved in useful activities that facilitate development, as well as prevent temptations of peer pressure. Provide youth with ideas of activities they can participate in outside of the home to keep them active and engaged. Most of our youth can easily engage in sports, club events, music, service learning, and faith activities.

Living in this era of time poverty and crisis, where parents are extremely busy, families must learn to manage life in harmony with what is truly most important. This necessitates open and ongoing communication. The family often provides the rudder that helps their kids hold to a course of responsible conduct even in the face of pressure from friends (Putnam 1996).

Consistent family meetings can help provide an anchor in the choppy water of life. Although it is optimal to develop this ritual when kids are young, it is never too late. Even teenagers can be compelled to attend if they feel appreciated and heard and are given some ownership for essential family decisions.

A family meeting's goals include acknowledging appreciations, preventing problems, and learning more about each other's feelings and expectations. Family meetings can also help organize the family's busy schedule.

You can create your list tailored to your family's needs; however, the following can serve as a guideline: Begin with appreciations and review times during the week when each youngster made a positive contribution to the family's welfare. Review and negotiate rules and consequences, allowing family members to provide input. Although the final decision will come from the parents, it is good to encourage a democratic atmosphere so that kids are prepared to thrive once they leave home. Themes for discussion during family meetings can include but not be limited to the following:

*Review the weekly schedule, as well as long-term

planning. Ensure that essential items (e.g., faith rituals, chores, leisure time) are preserved and prioritized. You may provide a weekly or monthly spending allowance to teach your kids about personal finance. You do not need to reward kids by paying them for chores. However, a monthly stipend may be useful, as it is good to let them have some responsibility for buying clothes, school supplies, etc., so that they are fiscally responsible later.

You might conclude your family meeting by discussing how you can take control of any stressors or reach out to others in need.

Some rules of a family meeting include:

*Be respectful of individual needs. For example, do not have a family meeting close to mealtime or bedtime. Turn the television and phone off during the session.

*Every family member is invited.

*Communication must be positive. There is to be no name-calling or yelling. Each member must show respect to everybody else.

*Family meetings are not a place to lecture. They are a place to discuss.

*Family members should try to see each other's point of view. Try not to be judgmental.

*The meetings should focus on family members' strengths and positive aspects of family life. It should be a time of problem-solving, not a gripe session.

Parents are the primary influence on their children's attitudes and behaviors. The positive influence of family activities cannot be overstated. Children and teenagers need to feel that they have a place in their families where they can be loved unconditionally yet are expected to contribute to others' welfare, including parents, siblings, friends, and community members.

Too many youngsters attribute poor choices to feeling bored. If kids do not have someone to share their worries, hopes, and dreams, they will often seek other fulfillment avenues. Constructive use of time involves shared activities that provide parents and children an atmosphere to work together and develop a mutual admiration and respect for each other. Often it is when you engage in the most meaningful conversations, which strengthens relationships. Furthermore, activities involving grandparents and other relatives can also be significant to facilitate growth and development.

Ongoing contact with extended family—children, parents, grandparents, aunts, uncles, and cousins—can help young people develop a sense of who they are, where they came from, and what they want to stand for.

All children are born to grow, develop, live, love, and articulate their needs and feelings for their self-protection, growth, and development. Every experience impacts brain development and functioning. A child's brain develops more than at any other time in life. And early brain development has a lasting impact on a child's ability to learn and succeed in school and life. The quality of a child's experiences in the first few years of life—positive or negative—helps shape how their brain develops.

We all want today's youth to thrive in life. So, we must ask, "How do we want our youth to act when they reach adulthood, and how do our educational efforts serve that end?" Competence and character seem the optimally desired outcome for youngsters to become life-learners and good citizens.

Ethical issues confront us every day. Many youngsters and adults adopt a live-and-let-live attitude about behavior: "I'll do what I want, and you do what you want. You don't judge me, and I won't judge you." Decision-making is reduced to risk/reward calculations. If the risk is low enough or the rewards are high enough, they can jettison ethical principles

and do what they think will benefit them immediately. Many people who cheat on exams, lie on resumes, or distort or falsify facts at work are never caught. So, the ethics of self-interest, at least in the short run, may seem to work. But the long-term risks are loss of trust, broken relationships, and loss of opportunities.

In his excellent book entitled *Instilling Touchstones of Character*, Dr. Gary Smit stated, "When we say someone has good character, we are expressing the opinion that his or her nature is defined by worthy traits, such as honesty, integrity, respect, responsibility, perseverance, and compassion. People of good character are guided by ethical principles even when physically dangerous or detrimental to their careers, social standing, or economic well-being. They do the right thing, even when it cost more than they want to pay."

Our interpersonal relationships are enriched when we genuinely care about another person's perspective and communicate in a manner that reflects a sense of caring, respect, and empathy, promoting excellent communication skills. "Your odds of being happy increase by 15 percent if a direct connection in your social network is happy. In other words, having direct and frequent social contact with someone who has high well-being dramatically boosts your chances of being happy" (Fredrickson 2009, 34).

Seemingly, actions speak louder than words, and many individuals who have a tremendous character do the right thing very quietly without a drumbeat. Their skills are often groomed when nobody is watching, regardless of the consequences of being tired or stressed. There is a vision for what they want from life and then an optimal direction for behavioral and attitudinal choices aided by continual self-evaluation.

What path do you know you want to take? There seems to be a plan and much motivation fueled by learning to enjoy the process and the present moments of unleashing talents and gifts in a meaningful fashion. The method of thriving in life will entail moments of fear and self-doubt.

This is normal and feeling anxious is not a sign of weakness. Our fight-or-flight response has been with us for thousands of years. However, our environments and threats to our well-being have changed significantly. The human mind has perhaps evolved in a manner to think negatively. Our brains are amazing but can serve as double-edged swords. The brain helps us analyze our world and generate ideas to thrive in life, such as innovating, self-evaluating, and being creative and adaptive. Conversely, our minds also have the potential to go to the dark side quickly by becoming overly critical and judgmental (Harris 2011).

Adverse childhood experiences are every day often

deemed traumatic. They can occur in clusters and contribute to high-risk health factors in adulthood: destructive behavior, depression, heart disease, cancer, or shortened life span. Stress and trauma increase inflammatory challenges within the body. What you do with your mind, combined with healthy relationships, impacts your psychological and physical health.

Sadly, many individuals will suffer from abandonment, rejection, and abuse. Hope becomes an antidote for traumatized individuals and provides a sense of freedom that the future can and will be better. Unwanted feelings are just a natural consequence of your entire body being exposed to distress. It is a part of the human experience that necessitates acceptance, followed by new skills to improve overall well-being, and eradicate shame and guilt. Being aware of present experience with approval, coupled with loving-kindness, self-compassion, and improved social support, has the potential to heal. The goal is to rid the thought that you are somehow defective but instead experienced an event or challenging period in life that shocked and slowed your bodily functions and healthy growth and development.

Being mindful and bored at the same time is nearly impossible. Focusing on your senses here and now appears to eradicate the psychological smog that contaminates happiness and planning for an optimal future. Being still may provoke feelings of change. Ironically, fear is not your enemy, and often is a friend tapping you on the shoulder, pleading for you to step out of your comfort zone.

Many conclude that high self-esteem, which entails a consistently positive evaluation of oneself and making and believing in positive statements and self-evaluation, is the correct path for sustained joy and happiness. How you go about  increasing your self-esteem or defining it can lead to a distorted sense of competence or, worse, a feeling that "I am better than others." We all have heard and may even know rock stars, movie stars, supermodels, and other famous people who are incredibly useful in perhaps one area but fall prey to a selfish and narcissistic belief system. Denying one's undercurrent of insecurities can lead to inauthenticity that will ultimately reveal itself and too often become devastating.

Adversity may strike at unexpected times regardless of your talent in one specific area of life. What matters most is the strength of your character and courage to seize opportunities to make the world a better place, even if it is one person at a time. Pay attention to how this makes you feel.

You likely realize that your life can be more meaningful, but there is no magical gimmick. If there were, eight billion individuals (and counting) on our earth would form an exceptionally long line for the mystical wisdom, or better yet, just one pill to swallow.

The world is not fair, and our ability to choose freely is overstated. We do not determine our genetic predispositions and our early experiences. Environments contaminated with toxic waste mixed with a lack of love, attachment, and security combined with losing genetics, impact individuals physically, emotionally, spiritually, and environmentally. Seemingly, we all must make the world a fair, just, and compassionate place.

Chapter 8

Jump-Starting Positive Changes

It is easier wanting to go on a diet when you have just eaten and are feeling full. The real challenge is making changes that are meaningful and sustained. The good news is that more exten-  sive and more transforming changes often begin with some shift, commonly referred to in contemporary research as shrinking change. Ultimately, the choices and resulting changes you make will likely need to be intrinsically motivating. "A well-established line of research shows that extrinsic rewards can undermine intrinsic motivation" (Peterson 2013, 186). Sadly, behaviors are often extinguished when external rewards are ended. That is why it is dangerous for parents to pay their children when they receive good grades.

You may jumpstart yourself by behavioral approaches and develop an elaborate reward system, but behaviors usually diminish unless they become an enjoyable lifetime endeavor. This is known as cognitive dissonance, the state of having inconsistent thoughts, beliefs, or attitudes, especially as relating to behavioral decisions and attitude change. Some examples of intrinsic motivation include participating in a sport because it is fun, and you enjoy it rather than doing it to win an award. Learning a new language because you like experiencing new things, not because your job requires it. Spending time with someone because you enjoy their company and not because they can further your social standing.

How have you made positive changes in the past? Have you ever wondered why it is so challenging to establish and sustain growth? It is often so easy to identify that a choice is not working. Most of us know that there will be consequences for not putting forth effort in school, eating poorly, drinking alcoholic beverages in excess, or breaking the law; many do the same thing repeatedly.

What are the ingredients that promote psychological health and move you closer to pursuing the good life? The following areas deserve our focus and are ripe for making useful choices.

*Love and close emotional attachment with others are vital for everyone to facilitate healthy development throughout the lifespan.

*Long-term stress, chaos, and abuse create stress hormones such as cortisol, which impede or damage the brain's healthy development.

*Children need to be allowed to explore their world in a safe fashion instead of being reprimanded for touching, moving, and sucking things.

*Discipline needs to be instructional when a youngster has the abstract ability to link choices and consequences. A proper balance of freedom and structure is crucial.

*Individuals can have cultural values that differ and make our world exciting, yet relationship skills seem to necessitate universal principles such as love, compassion, kindness, caring, respect, honesty, integrity, responsibility, fairness, and concern for others.

*Spirituality and faith can retain differing beliefs and hopefully help individuals become more proactive in genuinely loving their neighbors.

*Physical activity will become more critical concurrently with reducing time in a quiet place staring at a screen.

*Medical treatments, including medication, will increasingly become more effective at helping people feel better and relieve symptomology, but they can never replace loving relationships and healthy choices.

*Motivation is enhanced by focusing more on effort than the outcome.

*Developing a mindset of "I can" with effort is so much more powerful than "I can't do it because I have failed at this before."

*Relational skills need to be modeled and taught early, including bringing out the best in others with respect and gentleness, and eagerness to understand one another's perspective.

*Career development will necessitate clusters of multiple intelligences related to what someone enjoys doing, is good at, and has market demand.

*Choosing a lifelong partner for marriage needs more discernment and relational skill development.

*Short-term mood hits, such as alcohol, drugs, sex, overeating, and overspending, will almost always lead to undesirable consequences.

*Financial knowledge and willingness to live more frugally and simply will become more imperative, as debt can quickly get out of control and lead to chronic stress.

*Successful aging will be contingent on developing healthy communities that use an older person's wisdom to ensure life is always meaningful, and helps one feels significant.

*The world will continue to become more interconnected, and cooperation will be necessary to be good stewards of the universe.

*One must never retire from life and must keep trying to make the world a better place, one person at a time.

Any change is more sustainable when you have a firm and specific commitment concurrently with making intrinsically enjoyable choices. A mindset that focuses on effort, coupled with others' encouragement and accountability, also seems to be a facilitating force. Ironically, the motivation to "just do it" is good advice. Try to focus on a smaller change, which has more potential to begin the process of significant change effectively. You can surprise a loved one with a friendly letter. You can get out of workout clothes, put them next to your bed, and set the alarm for a morning workout. Once you are on your way, it takes more energy to turn back (Glasser 2011; Wubbolding 2010).

Change requires just doing something differently. Just think about the changes you have successfully made in the past.

Hope and optimism jumpstart change. You can imagine where you want to go and what works. Growth is also facilitated by knowing where you are going and why. This tends to quiet and relax the older brain, which generates good feelings. You can then focus more on effort (thoughts like "I can do it"), which is the mindset you need. It does help, however, to change your environment (e.g., get high-fat foods out of your home, have your workout clothes ready to go, etc.). You can build habits if you can maintain new behavior for at least thirty days. Many people often find it helpful to state their goals to keep them accountable; others like to journal, and some do both.

Ultimately change happens when you determine a specific want. This ignites internal motivation, which is necessary for sustaining movement toward a goal. We have much more control over our lives and choices than we realize. Choice theory and its delivery system—reality therapy—focus on taking control of choices linked to needs that appear to be genetically coded in your brain. You have a quality world (i.e., a vision of a good life) that serves as a picture album representing a collection of wants and desires. Your quality world may be somewhat vague or blurred when focused on just trying to survive the day. Your vision of a quality world is dynamic and can be changed, which is the impetus for writing this book, that is, to identify wants that are known to have a relationship to feeling good and being happy. You may want to improve your significant relationships, expand your support system, make more time for fun and enjoyment, learn new skills that are meaningful and challenging, change your current job situation, or just change your perception, so you appreciate what you already have. The WDEP system can be used over and over to get what you want in life. This acronym stands for the following:

W: exploring your wants, level of commitment, and internal control

D: exploring what you are doing to get what you want, including thinking, acting, feeling, and attending to your physiology and health

E: learning to self-evaluate the linkage to what you want, specific needs to be fulfilled, and effectiveness of overall direction related to identified wants and goals

P: continue making plans until eventually successful at achieving a goal (Wubbolding 2010).

Exploring and evaluating choices and consequences is vital to your success. Ask yourself: "Is what I am doing helping or hurting me?" "Is what I want attainable?" "Am I willing to expend the energy and effort to obtain what I want?" Additional questions that are useful include but are not limited to:

"Is the overall direction of my life getting me closer or further away from my specific goal?"

"Are my current choices bringing me closer or further away from the people who are important to me?"

"Are my current choices helping me or hurting me?"

"Do my current choices seem reasonable or unreasonable to others?"

"Are my self-statements effective or ineffective regarding optimal emotional consequences?"

"Does what I want at work align with the organization's vision and strategic plan?"

"Can I have full control of the choices I want to make?"

"Are my thoughts and action in harmony with my ethical values?"

"Is my current level of commitment enough to achieve my goal?"

"Is there a way I can shrink my goal to daily tasks that I know I can do?"

"Are my choices helping others as well as myself?"

Making positive changes is more comfortable when your plan is simple, attainable, measurable, and can be immediately implemented and controlled by you.

Knowing the good, loving the good, and doing the good necessitates greater awareness, motivation, and action to promote movement toward feeling good about your life.

The following attitudes and choices have the potential to help increase your wellness and help you pursue the good life.

Live Well:

Do you have a vision related to seeking a good life?

Do you take time to notice what is wonderful in life?

Can you welcome in the optimal amount of eustress to feel passionate about life?

Do you have the internal motivation to develop your wellness program, or do you have a wellness support and accountability system?

Are you engaged in a workout program that strengthens your entire muscle groups, improves your cardiovascular fitness, and appropriate stretching techniques?

Do you consistently self-evaluate what you want and the ultimate direction your choices are taking you?

Integrity with Relationships:

Do you give your loved ones time, attention, and affection?

Do you treat loved ones with admiration and fondness?

Do you avoid uncontrolled anger, contempt, stonewalling, and power and control?

Are you a good listener, and can you stay calm when the potential for conflict is high?

Have you developed rituals with loved ones to reflect on positive relationship memories?

Do you have an active spiritual or faith life to make your life more meaningful?

Do you have a plan to stretch your comfort zone and try to bring out the best in others, including yourself?

Finding Meaningful Work:

Do you fully understand and celebrate your unique intelligence?

Have you discovered a career and volunteer activities that utilize your gifts, talents, interests, and other priorities?

Do you work in an environment that brings out the best in you?

Have you discovered an optimal balance among

work, home, and leisure?

Are you disciplined regarding your finances?

Experiencing a Sense of Purpose:

Do you believe you are living a life that matters?

Do you live according to your ethical values?

Do you treat others the way they want to be treated?

Do you consistently try to bring out the best in others as well as yourself?

Are you making the world a better place?

Do you have a plan for what type of legacy you will leave the world?

Develop your bucket list of wants and then create a direction and plan to seize opportunities to make your hopes and dreams come true, with a constant emphasis on reflecting on and enjoying each present moment.

Chapter 9

Conclusion

Pursuing the good life necessitates creating an optimal vision and plan for satisfying the need for love, belonging, fun, freedom, and good health. The best way to experience feelings of pleasure, joy, and sustained happiness is to ensure that our behaviors and thoughts meet our needs in a useful fashion consistently. The following well-researched ways will increase your well-being:

*Having a sense of hope and optimism for the future

*Developing a vibrant social support network

*Challenging yourself in continuing education and work in an area of endeavor that matters to you

*Developing compelling goals concurrently with developing a capacity for delight and gratitude for all you have in the present moment

*Developing a sense of purpose and meaning in your life that is consistent with your values

*Seizing opportunities to be altruistic and bring out the best in others

*Engaging in regular physical activity and fueling the body by eating food that is high in nutritional value

*Taking time to be still and engaging in meditation, prayers, or any relaxation activity consistently throughout each day

The ultimate paradox is the more one tries to survive and play it safe in life, the more intense feelings of dissatisfaction often become the status quo, producing a constant hunger for some type of distraction to protect us from risking failure (Brach 2004; Carlson and Maniacci 2012). Fortunately, every moment provides us with opportunities to stretch our comfort zone, as all we have is the present moment.

You are benefited when you can take your wants and find a direction that gets you closer to fulfilling your basic needs. These needs likely entail receiving and giving love, feeling significant and empowered by unleashing your gifts and talents fueled by passion and fun, and having the freedom to do what you wish because you want to, not because of some type of external control.

The key is to do something different. The ultimate question is, can you harness and mobilize the process of change to move you closer to your vision of quality

CONCLUSION

life? Change is constant, inevitable, and part of everyone's life journey. Fortunately, positive changes can be set into motion by making just one shift in attitude or behavior. Please be reminded of the following: choices can only be made in the present. It is helpful to learn from the past, but do not be held hostage to it.

Furthermore, accept the future's uncertainty and focus on what you can control (Glasser 2012; Wubbolding 2010). The real test of pursuing higher states of well-being is to accept freedom of choice, especially when you do not want to. Your pursuit of the good life will be facilitated by the mindset, "With effort, I know I can do it!"

The candle of life is genuinely burning and a wonderful reminder that there is still a flame today, and all we have is the present moment. Your day can be illuminated by focusing on the following:

*Doing the right thing using trust, respect, responsibility, caring, and altruism to guide your choices.

*Improve our moral landscape by seizing opportunities to help others.

*Be reminded that healthy relationships are the key to experience sustained joy and happiness.

*Healthy relationships necessitate positivity, softening criticism and disrespectful behaviors, and the willingness to work through your problems and find solutions.

*Develop a capacity for delight by noticing what is right, good, and beautiful in life.

*Be aware that you have unique gifts and talents to

fuel your passion for getting you closer to what you want.

Seize opportunities to give each youngster time, affection, and attention.

*Be reminded that you need love, belonging, significance, fun, freedom, and good health.

*Keep hope alive, be willing to do something different, and develop healthy mini habits that will ultimately transform your life.

*Enjoy the journey and set yourself up to have the best day possible!

Your life is a precious gift. The combination of being grateful for what is going right and having a sense of hope and encouragement to stretch your comfort zone is powerful. As a result of your legacy, the world will be a better place because of your positive energy, loving-kindness, and using your skills and talents in a meaningful fashion.

It has been said, "The pain of regret is far greater than the pain of self-discipline." I believe that to be true. Your life story is unfolding, and I appreciate being a facilitating force on your journey.

Thank you for all you have done to make our world a better place by seizing opportunities to bring out the best in yourself and others. Be well, my friend, and best to you as you pursue the good life!

CONCLUSION

References

Anchor, Shawn (2013). *The Happiness Advantage*. New York: Crown Publishing Group.

Ben-Shahar, Tal (2007). *Happier*. New York: McGraw-Hill.

Brach, Tara (2004). *Radical Acceptance: Embracing Your Life with the Heart of Buddha*. New York: Bantam Books.

Britzman, Mark, and W. Hanson (2005). *What Every Educator and Youth Leader Must Know: The Case for Character Education and CHARACTER COUNTS!* Los Angeles: Josephson Institute of Ethics.

Brooks, David, and Goble, Frank (1997). *The Case for Character Education*. Northridge, CA: Studio 4 Productions.

Cameran, Julia (2012). *The Prosperous Heart*. New York: Penguin Books.

Carlson, Jon, and Maniacci, Michael, P. (2012). *Alfred Adler Revisited*. New York: Routledge.

Carlson, Richard (1998). *Do Not Sweat the Small Stuff at Work: Simple Ways to Minimize Stress and Conflict While Bringing out the Best in Yourself and Others*. New York: Hyperion.

Carroll, P. & Gervais, P. (2020). *Compete to Create: An Approach to Living and Leading Authentically*. Audible Originals.

Covey, Stephen (2006). *Everyday Greatness*. Nashville: Rutledge Hill Press.

Declaire, Joan, and Gottman, John (2006). *Ten Lessons to Transform Your Marriage: America's Love Lab Experts Share Their Strategies on How to Improve Your Relationship*. New York: Random House, Inc.

Dweck, Carol (2007). *Mindset: The New Psychology of Success*. New York: Random House, Inc.

Louv, Richard (2008). *Last Child in the Woods*. New York: Workman Publishing.

Forsyth, John P., and Georg H. Eifert (2007). *The Mindfulness & Acceptance Workbook for Anxiety*. Oakland, CA: New Harbinger Publications, Inc.

Fredrickson, Barbara. (2009). *Positivity*. New York: Crown Publishers.

Gardner, Howard (2011). *Frames of Mind: The Theory of Multiple Intelligences*. New York: Basic Books.

Glasser, William (2011). *Take Charge of Your Life: How to Get What You Want with Choice Theory Psychology*. Bloomington, IN: iUniverse, Inc.

Glasser, William, and Glasser, Carleen (2007). *Eight Lessons for a Happier Marriage*. New York: HarperCollins Publishers.

Goleman, Daniel (2006). *Emotional Intelligence*. New York: Bantam Books.

Gottman, John (2011). *The Seven Principles for Making Marriage Work: A Practical Guide from the Country's Foremost Relationship Expert*. New York: Three Rivers Press.

Haidt, Johnathan (2006). *The Happiness Hypothesis*. New York: Basic Books.

Hanson, Richard (2013). *Hardwiring Happiness*. New York: Harmony.

Harris, Richard (2011). *The Confidence Gap: A Guide to Overcoming Fear and Self-Doubt*. Boston: Trumpeter Books.

Henry, Todd (2013). *Die Empty: Unleash Your Best Work Every Day*. New York: Penguin Group.

Lake, Gina (2013). *From Stress to Stillness: Tools for Inner Peace*. Sedona, AZ: Endless Satsang Foundation.

Lapine, Phoebe (2017). *The Wellness Project. How I Learned to Do Right by My Body, Without Giving My Life*. New York: Penguin Random House.

Lickona, Thomas (1992). *Educating for Character: How Our Schools Can Teach Respect and Responsibility*. Washington, DC: Character Education Partnership.

Lickona, Thomas and Matt Davidson (2005). *Smart & Good High Schools: Integrating Excellence and Ethics for Success in School, Work, and Beyond*. Cortland, NY: Center for the 4th and 5th R's. Washington, DC: Character Education Partnership.

Locke, John (1689). 1975 *Essay Concerning Human Understanding*. Oxford: Clarendon Press. Book 2, Chapter 21, Section 51., Peter H. Nidditch, ed. of reprinted book.

Lyumbomirsky, Sonja (2007). *The How of Happiness: A Scientific Approach to Getting the Life You Want*. New York: The Penguin Press.

Markman, Howard, Stanley, Scott, Blumberg, Susan (2010). *Fighting for Your Marriage: A Deluxe Revised Edition of the Classic Best Seller for Enhancing Marriage and Preventing Divorce*. San Francisco: Jossey-Bass.

Meyers, David G. (1992). *The Pursuit of Happiness*. New York: Avon Books.

Meyers, David G. (2000). *The American Paradox: Spiritual Hunger in An Age of Plenty*. New Haven, CT: Yale University Press.

Miller, William and Rollnick, Stephen (2002). *Motivational Interviewing*. New York: Guildford Press.

Oettingen, Gabriele (2014). *Rethinking Positive Thinking*. New York: Penguin Group.

Peterson, Christopher (2013). *Pursuing the Good Life: 100 Reflections on Positive Psychology*. Oxford: Oxford University Press.

Putnam, Robert (2001). *Bowling Alone: The Collapse and Revival of The American Community*. New York: Simon & Schuster

Rath, Tom (2007). *Strengthfinder 2.0*. New York: Gallup Press.

Rath, Tom (2013). *Eat Move Sleep: Why Small Changes Lead to Big Differences*. Arlington, VA: Missionday

Rath, Tom and Harter, Jim (2010). *Well Being: The Five Essential Elements*. New York: Gallup Press.

Ricard, Matthieu (2011). *Happiness*. New York: Little, Brown and Company.

Siegel, Dan (2011). *Mindsight: The New Science of Personal Transformation*. New York: Bantam Books.

Smit, Gary (2014). *Instilling Touchstones of Character*. College Station, TX: Virtualbookworm.com Publishing, Inc.

Southwick, Steven and Charney, Dennis (2012). *Resilience: The Science of Mastering Life's Greatest Challenges*. Cambridge: Cambridge University Press.

Tileston, Donna (2004). *What Every Teacher Should Know About Student Motivation*. Thousand Oaks, CA: Corwin Press.

US Department of Health and Human Services and US Department of Agriculture. 2015–2020 *Dietary Guidelines for Americans*. 8th Ed., December 2015.

Wehrenberg, Margaret (2008). *The 10 Best-Ever Anxiety Management Techniques*. New York: W.W. Norton & Company.

Wubbolding, Robert (2010). *Reality Therapy*. Washington, DC: American Psychological Association.

Dr. Mark J. Britzman

Pursuing the Good Life: Counseling and Consulting, LLC

www.pursingthegoodlife.com

About the Author

Dr. Mark J. Britzman, Ed.D. is a licensed psychologist and practices in the Black Hills of South Dakota. He provides counseling to individuals, couples, and families; and is a nationally recognized speaker in promoting psychological health, marital preparation, and character education.

Mark was chosen as an International William Glasser Scholar and received advanced training and certification in choice theory/reality therapy to ensure that he can keep his counseling skills at a high level and integrate new research to help others in a pragmatic and meaningful fashion.

Mark is a former tenured professor in counselor education. He received the South Dakota Counseling Association's highest award for service to his field and the Outstanding Teaching, Advising and Research Awards in the College of Education and Human Science at South Dakota State University.

Please consider going to the website, www.pursuingthegoodlife.com, and signing up to receive Mark's blogs and exchange wisdom and encouragement with each other.

Pursuing the Good Life
Your Life Assessment
Dr. Mark J. Britzman, Ed.D.©

Name:

What are you doing when you feel more energetic and passionate about your life?

When do you feel most grateful for what is happening in your life?

What helps you do the right thing?

What helps inspire you to be a better person?

What do you value the most in your life?

How would you describe your life philosophy?

What positive attributes have helped you produce quality results?

What helps you remain optimistic that something good might happen soon?

How have you overcome adversity in the past?

If you had more courage, how would your life be different?

What are your more predominant regrets in life thus far?

What is your greatest fear in life going forward?

How are you overly hard on yourself?

How much control do you believe you have to improve your life?

What gives your life more spiritual meaning?

What gives your life a more profound purpose?

How are you able to change your focus to the present moment?

If your life story is currently captured in a book, what would the title be?

What do you want to happen in the next chapter of your life story?

What is your current plan and direction to get closer to what you want in life?

What helps you or hinders you from living a life that matters?

www.ingramcontent.com/pod-product-compliance
Lightning Source LLC
Chambersburg PA
CBHW061203070526
44579CB00010B/119